LEARN TO WRITE THE HEBREW SCRIPT

*Aleph Through the Looking Glass*

LEARN TO WRITE THE HEBREW SCRIPT

*Aleph Through the Looking Glass*

JONATHAN ORR-STAV

Yale University Press

New Haven and London

All illustrations are by the author unless otherwise stated.

Publisher: Mary Jane Peluso
Manuscript Editor: Ann-Marie Imbornoni
Production Controller: Maureen Noonan
Cover Designer: Mary Valencia
Editorial Assistant: Brie Kluytenaar
Marketing Manager: Timothy Shea

Printed in the United States of America

Library of Congress Cataloging-in-Publication Data
Lotan, Jonathan
[From A to aleph]
   Learn to write the Hebrew script : aleph through the looking glass / Jonathan Orr-Stav.
p. cm.
       Originally published under title: From A to aleph
       Includes bibliographical references and index.
ISBN 0-300-10841-9 (alk. paper)
 ISBN 0-300-11334-X (pbk. : alk. paper)
          1. Hebrew language—Writing. I. Title.

    PJ4589.L68 2006
    492.4'82421—dc22

2005042603

A catalogue record for this book is available from the British Library.

10  9  8  7  6  5  4  3  2  1

To Ethan and Guy

(You'll be tested on this.)

*And the whole earth was of one language, and of one speech. And it came to pass as they journeyed from the east, that they found a plain in the land of Shin'ar, and they dwelt there. And they said one to another, Go to, let us make brick, and burn them thoroughly. And they had brick for stone, and slime had they for mortar. And they said, Go to, let us build us a city and a tower, whose top may reach unto heaven; and let us make us a name, lest we be scattered abroad upon the face of the whole earth.*

*And the Lord came down to see the city and the tower, which the children of men builded. And the Lord said, Behold, the people is one, and they have all one language, and this they begin to do: and now nothing will be restrained from them, which they have imagined to do. Go to, let us go down, and there confound their language, that they may not understand one another's speech. So the Lord scattered them abroad from thence upon the face of all the earth: and they left off to build the city. Therefore is the name of it called Babel; because the Lord did there confound the language of all the earth: and from thence did the Lord scatter them abroad upon the face of all the earth.*

(Genesis 11:1-9)

# Contents

## A Guide to the Perplexed

The words *Roman* and *script* have different meanings to the typographer as opposed to the historian or layman. To avoid confusion, in this book **Roman** (with a capital *R*) refers to the script of Western European languages, while **roman** (lowercase) denotes its typographical meaning of the default upright style of a typeface (as distinct from its *italic* form).

Similarly, the word *script* (lowercase) alludes to the general writing system of a given language or culture, while references to *Script* – with capital *S* – will be in its typographical sense of a typeface where letters *are consistently joined up* (vs. *cursive*, say, where they're not).

In keeping with the general theme of this book, Hebrew words are transliterated primarily according to  visual rather than linguistic considerations, the better to condition the reader's eye to the graphic forms of Hebrew spelling. In most cases this coincides with linguistic conventions and historical origins, with one notable exception: the Hebrew letter *caf* (*kaf*) is represented here by the Roman *c* rather than the traditional (and historically correct) *k*. Furthermore, I use *ç* to designate the "soft" *caf* (pronounced like the Scottish *ch* as in *loch*). This was done in order to exploit the coincidental but compelling resemblance between *kaf* and *c*, and as a convenient shorthand for the soft version, without resorting to combinations such as *kh* or the more ambiguous *ch*. Finally, small caps are used to indicate instances of the guttural letter *Het* (pron. like *ch* in *Bach* or *loch*) and of the letter *Tet*, to distinguish between them and the letters *héh* and *tav*, respectively.

Your indulgence is appreciated.

## Acknowledgments

I am indebted to the following:

- Rivka Gonen, Itaï Tamari, Melanie Garson (separately), and to Amatzia Porat of the Academy of the Hebrew Language, for pointing me in the right direction at various junctures of my research; and to Natan Nahmias, for same and for valuable tips on ancient Hebrew pronunciation

- Rivka Plesser, at The Jewish National & University Library, Jerusalem, for attentive and invaluable help in procuring various illustrations

- Ilana Tahan, Hebrew Curator at the British Library Oriental & India Collection, for similar help in London

- The Bodleian Library (Oxford), for permission to reproduce certain texts

- My aunt, Miriam Eliav-Feldon, for unwittingly getting the ball rolling all those years ago, and more recently for access to the family archives and help and comments on various Renaissance and Reformation sources

- Ada Yardeni for her inspiring work on the development of the Hebrew script down the ages, and for her personal encouragement and permission to use her illustrations

- Bairbre O'Malley, Valerie Evans, Shirley Bygott, and others who helped test the method in its early days; Donatella, Diana, and the gang at the Hebrew classes of London University's School of Oriental & African Studies for acting as the unwitting control group

- Last but not least, my mother, Yael Lotan, for teaching me most of what I know about English and about writing; for reviewing and editing the manuscript early on for readability and style; and for serving as a tireless sounding board throughout.

◊

# Introduction

## The why

Mastering a new language is always a challenge. This is doubly true when you venture into a different family of languages from those which you already know. Throw in a different script as well, however, and you feel you're losing contact with solid ground.

As a Semitic tongue that shares its script with no other living language, Hebrew unfortunately scores on all three counts for the typical Westerner. Historians may find it intriguing that the Hebrew script is the only surviving writing system of antiquity that is still unique to a single national entity, but to students of Hebrew as a Foreign Language (HFL), it is only a complication they could do well without.

Just how daunting it is to be confronted by a totally unfamiliar script is something I suspect designers of most conventional HFL courses are not fully aware of. Hebrew is usually their native language, and the Roman script is also familiar to them from childhood through continual exposure on billboards, and in books, the media, and of course school. For the typical HFL student, however, the sight of the Hebrew script makes the expression "It looks Greek to me" sound positively wistful. For their sake, it seems to me, one should strive to make the task as easy as

1

possible, even if it means departing somewhat from tradition.

With this appreciation in mind I set out to produce this book. I have a slightly unusual perspective in that my introduction to the language was different from that of both native Israelis and most new immigrants. I was born outside Israel to a born-and-bred Jerusalemite who, homesick after fifteen years abroad, returned to her homeland and family with my sister and me in tow. I was ten at the time: young enough to learn quickly, but old enough to experience and remember the difficulties all new immigrants face when encountering the Hebrew script for the first time. With the benefit of a native-speaking mother and extended family, however, I never had to attend special Hebrew-learning classes (*ulpan*).

Instead, my education in this field began, at my instigation, the morning after our arrival. Anxious to impress my mother with a quick mastery of the language, I asked her sister (then a university student) to teach me. Caught unawares, my aunt Miri grabbed the nearest children's book to hand – the Hebrew version of *Peter and the Wolf* – sat me down, and proceeded to teach me both language and script, word by word. I knew nothing of either, so it wasn't an easy introduction, but thanks to her patient efforts and the subsequent support of the extended family, I eventually caught up with my native classmates and was promoted to the highest stream of Hebrew studies three years later. Nevertheless, I know now that the task would have been much easier had I had access to the method I describe below.

Ironically, the clues to the Three Steps method set out here were given to me by my grandfather some three years after our arrival in the country, when I no longer needed them. But I had the satisfaction of seeing the technique they ultimately inspired vindicated years later, following a party with British friends in London, when I dismissed the notion that the script was intimidating. "I could probably teach you the knack of writing in Hebrew in three lessons – in as many weeks," I told them, with the brash confidence of a twenty-something. Three of them took me up on it, and happily, on this particular youthful boast, I was able to deliver.

In fact, the exercise succeeded beyond my expectations. After the third lesson, not only were my friends able to write their names and simple words in Hebrew characters, but their handwriting was noticeably superior to that of a typical *ulpan* student: letters such as *shin* and *lamed*, for example, were written as they should be, instead of as approximate versions of an italic *e* and the Greek *∂*, respectively, as is usually the case with students of the language. This confirmed my hope that with the Three Steps method, their hands were working "with the grain" of the script instead of fighting against it.

Encouraged by this and by the surprising degree of interest I found among Jews and non-Jews alike in the subject, I began researching the literature for books based on these ideas, convinced that they must exist. When, to my amazement, I found none, I decided to develop the concept into a consistent method and write such a book for the benefit of a wider audience. When the opportunity arose in 1995 (in between writing books on computer-aided design), I did.

**The wherefore**

The central premise behind *Learn to Write the Hebrew Script* is that, unlike the language itself, the Hebrew script is not nearly as foreign as one is usually led to believe. It shares significant common ground with its European counterparts – one that, properly tapped, can provide the Western student with a tremendous leg-up and a familiar frame of reference. Thanks to the findings of modern archaeology, this common history is now quite well understood, and possessing even a cursory knowledge of this pays big dividends.

As we shall see, understanding the implications of the switch in the direction of writing made by the ancient Greeks around 500 BCE leads not only to an appreciation of why Hebrew characters are the way they are, but *to a natural inclination to write them that way.* Exercises with one's own native writing in Roman characters naturally make the learning process that much easier and the retention more effective.

With the skill of writing, of course, comes much of the ability to read. Once you master the Hebrew cursive, it is but a short step to conquering the traditional "Square" form in which the language is normally printed. You can thus make good headway in this area without ever having to grapple with the intricacies of Hebrew grammar or vocabulary. Yet, because the language and script are so intimately intertwined, by the time you have completed or even perused the Three Steps, you will find you have absorbed many aspects of the language almost unconsciously. This book can therefore serve not only as an amusing pastime but also as a useful complement to traditional HFL textbooks.

**Breaking with tradition**

It is important, though, to note that the Three Step approach departs from traditional HFL teaching methods on three important counts:

1.  It teaches the skill of writing in Hebrew script separately from the language itself. In the conventional approach, which binds the teaching of Hebrew script tightly with that of reading, grammar, and vocabulary in one integrated package, this is considered a highly unorthodox, not to say outlandish, notion.

2.  It introduces the Hebrew alphabet through its modern cursive forms rather than the traditional Square forms of most printed texts. This, too, may raise some eyebrows, since the modern cursive is a comparatively recent phenomenon, and the overwhelming majority of Hebrew in print is in the Square form.

3.  Last but not least, it highlights and celebrates the historical kinship between the Hebrew alphabet and European scripts rather than ignoring or denying it. Traditional methods prefer to present the Hebrew script much as if it were Chinese or Korean, i.e., as something utterly unrelated to European alphabets. Hebrew letters are taught on a seemingly arbitrary, take-it-or-leave-it basis – the *this is an aleph don't ask why* approach. Sharp-eyed students who spot suspicious similarities between certain Hebrew characters and their Roman or Cyrillic or Greek counterparts are actively discouraged from pursuing this line of thinking any further on the grounds that such similarities are – in the manner of disclaimers at the end of Hollywood film credits – entirely coincidental and unintentional.

As we shall see, such objections owe more to a preference to let sleeping dogs lie, to honest ignorance, and to historical circumstance than to any objective comparison of effectiveness. Archaeological discoveries of the past hundred years or so in fact provide clear clues to a "map" by which the modern reader might navigate from the Roman script to Hebrew writing with little resort to arbitrary learning by rote. There is also unimpeachable institutional support for what I am proposing here, namely, that the skill of writing Hebrew can and even should be taught separately from the skill of reading it – particularly when teaching adults – and that the Hebrew script should be introduced to such students through the activity of writing cursive rather than Square letters.[1]

The real proof, of course, is in the pudding. The results of informal experiments with my non-Hebrew-speaking friends have been encouraging. In the spirit of those live lessons, this volume is designed to be read on the train or bus, or in a dentist's waiting room, rather than at a desk. Even the exercises are intended more as doodles to engage in while on the phone rather than as sit-down "homework." Like riding a bicycle or typing, writing in Hebrew is a skill that you can acquire incrementally, never really lose, and continually improve, at your own pace and with your own material, as and when the opportunity arises.

Remember: this book is about writing *in* Hebrew, as opposed to writing Hebrew in the proper literary sense, which of course requires knowledge of the language and is an art in itself, much as writing in any language. If this strikes you as disappointing – or worse, as a legalistic nicety – bear in mind that many modern Hebrew words are merely transliterations of familiar European ones. Most – such as *informatziah, telefon, otobus, qonteqst, alternativah,* and less academic but charming examples such as *beck-ex* (rear axle) and *front beck-ex* (front axle) – are modern innovations. Others – such as *cartis* (card), *avir* (air), *basis* (basis/base), and *itztadyon* (stadium) – have been around for over two thousand years, having been drawn directly from classical Greek before any modern European language was a twinkle in a legionnaire's eye.

Thus modern Hebrew speakers, not unlike their English-speaking counterparts, often have the luxury of choice from two parallel lexicons – one native, one Latin/Greek – with all the richness and versatility that this provides.* Thus, *informatziah* is also *meida, qonteqst = heqsher, emotzionali = rigshi, alternativah = halufah,* and so on. For our purposes, the existence of such European words and their usually Italian-like declension means that, as a Western reader, you are unwittingly already in pos-

---

\* A distinction is made by some Jews in the Diaspora between *Hebrew* and *Ivrit* ("Hebrew" in Hebrew) – meaning biblical Hebrew and modern Hebrew, respectively. This suggests that they are distinct languages, like Greek and ancient Greek – which is puzzling to a modern Israeli, as this simply isn't the case. Native Hebrew speakers make no such distinction, just as English speakers do not employ a different word to distinguish the English of Shakespeare from that of today. The innovations of modern Hebrew are merely extensions to the same edifice – not replacements. Israeli schoolchildren generally have little difficulty understanding the Old Testament as is; its constructions are the final arbiter in deciding correct modern usage; and when reading the books of Exodus, Samuel, or Kings, one is repeatedly struck by how little the nation's speech has changed, in word or in manner, in over three thousand years.

session of a wealth of examples with which to try out your Hebrew-writing skills as you go along (in addition to those in the text and in the appendix). Another reason for giving them prominence here is that their spelling follows simple and consistent phonetic rules that are easily mastered and set out in the Three Steps – unlike native Hebrew words, whose correct spelling often requires knowledge of their grammatical root, which is beyond the scope of this book.

As I said, this book is for all levels and types of interest. If you are a serious student of the language, you will need to supplement it with standard HFL textbooks on grammar and the like, but it should nevertheless give you a useful leg-up and some handy insights and, above all, dispel much of the intimidating mystique surrounding the subject. If your interest is more casual, and even if you never practice the exercises, you will at least have learned some interesting pointers about the evolution of a fairly critical aspect of Western civilization (the debate of the People's Front of Judea in Monty Python's *Life of Brian* as to the mutual benefits of the relationship between Rome and Judea will never be quite the same again).

Last but not least, you'll have some good dinner party material and be able to strike awe and wonder in friends and family alike with your ability to jot down their names in the language of the Old Testament.

Good luck, and above all – enjoy!

◊

# Part I

*A Brief History of (Western) Writing*

## Why the Hebrew Script Isn't

### For those in a hurry

True to this book's title, you don't have to read this chapter if all you want to do is master the skill of writing in Hebrew characters.

If talk of ancient history, Middle Eastern empires, and the like puts you to sleep – skim through it, use it as a standby against insomnia, or skip it and move on to Part II, which deals with the actual Three Steps. All the essential tips you need are spelled out there. But if you have the time and patience, I'd recommend sticking around. The backdrop to this story is a rattling good yarn, if only because so few people seem to know it, and because it hauls out of the closet one or two things that look suspiciously like skeletons. It also explains the theoretical principles behind the Three Steps method, which are interesting in themselves.

### Write like an Egyptian

Most people never really ask themselves where Western writing actually comes from. They know that the alphabet we use today was created by the Romans (with the exception of letters such as *J*, *U*, and *W*, which were formalized later), and that their alphabet was in turn based upon that of the ancient Greeks – but beyond that it goes all hazy. Since classical Greece is usually regarded as the fount of all Western civilization, the average North American or European of today assumes that its alphabet sprang fully formed from its rocky soil, like the warrior-founders of

11

Sparta from the dragon teeth planted by Cadmus. Meanwhile, students of Hebrew as a Foreign Language (HFL) are taught the Hebrew script as if it were something entirely unrelated to the writing you are reading now – which makes it very daunting.

Both attitudes are misguided, for there is a clear historical link between the Hebrew and European alphabets that can greatly help natives of both to bridge the gap between them. This connection was largely forgotten in the Christian era and has been only recently uncovered by archaeologists and paleographers through various finds, starting with the discovery and deciphering of the Rosetta Stone in Egypt some two hundred years ago. In my case, it was only thanks to my grandfather – a sometime student of Semitic languages – that my attention was drawn, as a boy, to the fact that the very word *alphabet* is derived from the old Phoenician/Hebrew names for the first two letters (*aleph, bet*), as indeed are the names of most Greek letters.

He also showed me some of the better-known examples of this evolution, such as how the original ancient Egyptian hieratic (the cursive form of hieroglyphics) for an ox (Fig. 1-a) was adopted around 1500 BCE by the Canaanites (linguistically, the group comprising Phoenicians, Israelites, Moabites, and all other Western Semitic peoples in the areas of modern-day Lebanon, Syria, Israel, and Jordan), who turned it on its side and named it after the Semitic word for ox – *aluph* or *aleph (*Fig. 1-b*)*. Several hundred years later, he explained, the ancient Greeks adopted it, too, turning it yet another 90° and renaming it *alpha* (Fig. 1-c).

a b c

Fig. 1 The hieratic for "ox" (a), the Canaanite *aleph* (b), and the ancient Greek
*alpha*

Other Egyptian signs were similarly transformed – thus, the hieratic
for "water" (Fig. 2-a) became the Canaanite sign *mem* (Fig. 2-b), meaning the same thing. This later became the Greek and Roman letter *M*,
and so on.

a b

Fig. 2 The hieratic for "water" (a) and the Old Hebrew/Phoenician *mem* (b)

This brief glimpse into the evolution of writing left me thunder-
struck and entranced. Once pointed out, it seemed so obvious and compelling, I assumed it must be common knowledge. However, years later, I
learned that far from being exploited as an aid in teaching Hebrew to
nonnative speakers, the very fact that the scripts of ancient Egypt,
Canaan, and Europe are related in any way is either unknown or actively
suppressed outside the specialist field of Near East archaeology and
related academic fields. Even in modern Israel, familiarity with the forms

13

of ancient Hebrew writing (as opposed to the language itself) is virtually nonexistent outside these circles.

## A mutually convenient silence

There is no official explanation that I am aware of for this widespread ignorance of the historical kinship of these scripts, but it is not difficult to surmise.

One reason may be the uneasy, at times downright hostile, relationship between Christians and Jews for most of the past two millennia. Portraying the opposing culture as something entirely alien made it easier for both parties to discourage their followers from excessive interest in the other. Admittedly, Hebrew has always played an important role in the study of early Christianity, but it was the language of the Old Testament (as opposed to the New, which was Greek), and its linguistic and alphabetic differences made it a convenient symbol, for anyone so inclined, of the contrasts between Judaism and Christianity, Asia and Europe, Semitic and European. Thus, any memory of the common ancestry of the Hebrew and European alphabets that might have lingered during Roman times was played down and ignored by Christians until eventually it was forgotten. This denial suited Orthodox Jewry, too, as it helped to maintain its barriers against outside influences. Both parties thus perpetuated and widened a largely imaginary divide.

Even today, and particularly in circles more favorably disposed toward Judaism – especially mysticism, popular Kabbala, etc. – there is little desire to discover that Hebrew and European scripts have a shared

14

ancestry. After all, the power of the Hebrew alphabet lies precisely in its exotic quality: if it transpires that it is a mere cousin of the mundane letters of daily newspapers and graffiti throughout the Western world, its aura of mystique goes right out the window. So, too, do mythic images of Moses and the Tablets as portrayed in paintings such as Rembrandt's *Moses Smashes the Stone Tablets with the Text*, where the Ten Commandments are spelled out in the square letters of medieval and modern Hebrew.[2]

A similar reluctance to acknowledge the kinship of Hebrew to European scripts can be seen in the writings of medieval Christian Hebrew scholars, whose preoccupation with the exotic in Hebrew typography of the period (thicker horizontals than verticals, the literal square template) often exceeded the care required to distinguish between similar-looking Hebrew characters. Indeed, their delight in stressing such superficial stylistic features often led to heavily flawed or downright misleading rendition of several characters, betraying a fundamental ignorance of the basic forms of the Hebrew alphabet. There certainly appears to be no awareness that it shares a common ancestry with the Roman or Greek characters of the main text (Fig. 3).

**The best kept secret**

All of which brings us to the most interesting but least known argument against linking the scripts of the Old Testament and the New, namely that what we commonly have known as the Hebrew script for over two thousand years is not the original Hebrew script at all, but a

15

more distant cousin.

It is in fact a late variety of Aramaic. Originally the language of the Assyrians to the north and northeast of the Israelite kingdoms, Aramaic is closely related to Hebrew and Phoenician but was initially written in the cuneiform script of Mesopotamia. Around 1000 BCE, however, this was discarded in favor of the script common throughout Canaan.

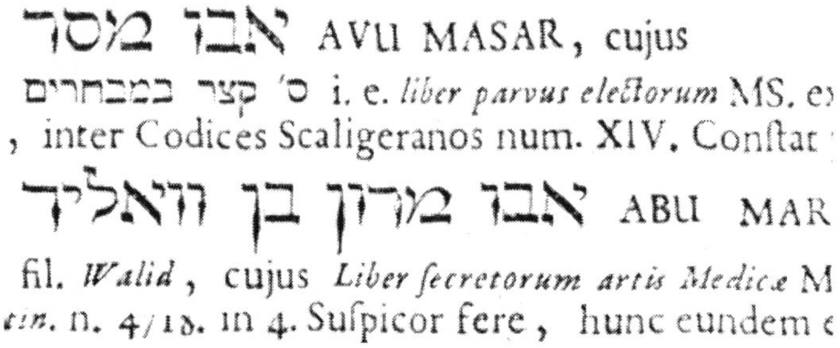

אבו מסר AVU MASAR, cujus
ס' קצר במבחרים i. e. *liber parvus electorum* MS. e)
, inter Codices Scaligeranos num. XIV. Conftat
אבו מרון בן ואליד ABU MAR
fil. *Walid*, cujus *Liber fecretorum artis Medicæ* M
*cm.* n. 4/13. in 4. Sufpicor fere, hunc eundem c

Fig. 3 The traditional European view of the Hebrew alphabet is apparent in this sixteenth-century German volume on Hebrew authors and writings (Reprinted from Wolf 1527, p. A-3).

This proved to be a wise move; the Canaanite script was vastly more effective than cuneiform, and with a few tweaks to make the forms more regular and distinctive from one another, it outlived the Assyrian empire to become the chosen medium of administration of the two empires that succeeded it: Babylon and Persia. Over five hundred years of such intensive use, the Aramaic script, as it became known, diverged noticeably from its Canaanite origins, even though in name and function the characters remained the same.

16

## Hebrew vs. Aramaic

Despite its success at the imperial level, the Aramaic script was never contemplated as a medium for depicting Hebrew until around 520 BCE, when the Persian emperor Cyrus allowed Jews to return to Judea from exile in Babylon.

Although they had spent only seventy-five years in exile – a mere walk in the park compared to the Second Exile that was to come – the returning Judeans were almost unseemly in their rush to dump the ancestral Hebrew script in favor of that of its imperial cousin. They were clearly impressed by life in the Babylonian capital, and as descendants of the exiled Judean aristocracy and intelligentsia, they were keenly aware of their social status in relation to "the poor of the land" who had never left (II Kings 25:12) and apparently regarded most things local – ancestral script included – as socially and culturally inferior.

To the modern reader, however – in both Israel and the West – the original Hebrew script is a revelation. Certain characters (*aleph, héh, ayin*) were co-opted by the Greeks to represent European vowels, while others (*Tet, sammeç, tzadi*) were dropped altogether by Roman times. The remainder, however, still bear a striking resemblance to the mirror images of their ancient and even modern Greek and Roman counterparts nearly three thousand years later (Fig. 4). The same cannot be said about the Aramaic script that the Jews brought back with them from Babylon.

There followed a process lasting a good two hundred years or more, during which the Old Hebrew script (known as *ctav ivri*) fought valiantly to stand its ground against the new pretender, known as *ctav ashuri* (liter-

17

ally, Assyrian script). Gradually, under a policy of deliberate neglect by the ruling and rabbinical authorities, the Old Hebrew alphabet died out. The final nail in the coffin came when, in the late third century BCE, it was passed over in favor of the Aramaic script by the Sanhedrin (rabbinical assembly) as its script of choice for the biblical canon then being compiled and transcribed. To downplay the historic significance of what they were doing, its name was changed, too, from *ctav ashuri* to the more neutral *ctav meruba* (Square script), by which name it is still known today.

The decision to replace the Old Hebrew script with the Aramaic one was extraordinary. For the administration of the new Persian province of *Yehud* (Judea), the use of Aramaic language and script in matters of state was to be expected. But that the same script was used to provide the official written record of the biblical canon and of the debates of the Talmudic assemblies in place of the one used by Moses, David, and Solomon is astonishing. Not for nothing is it one of the best kept secrets in history.

Today such a move would be unthinkable. In the 1960s, for example, a public outcry in Israel forced the venerable Academy of the Hebrew Language – the nation's premier arbiter on all matters relating to Hebrew – to back down from a tentative proposal merely to introduce two new signs – representing the vowels *a* and *e* – into the alphabet to enhance the readability of foreign words and names without the use of dots and dashes normally used for this purpose (more of which later).

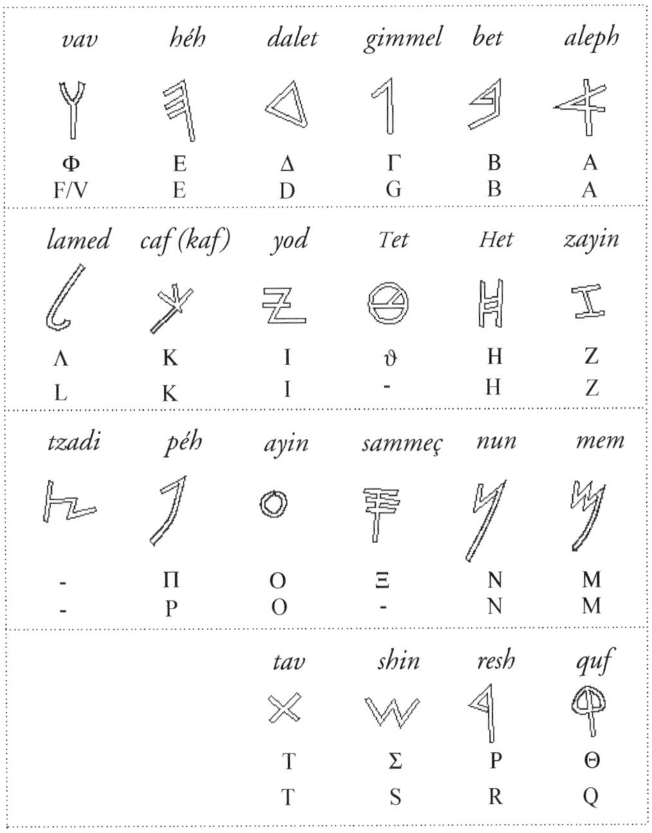

| vav | héh | dalet | gimmel | bet | aleph |
|-----|-----|-------|--------|-----|-------|
| Φ | E | Δ | Γ | B | A |
| F/V | E | D | G | B | A |

| lamed | caf (kaf) | yod | Tet | Het | zayin |
|-------|-----------|-----|-----|-----|-------|
| Λ | K | I | ϑ | H | Z |
| L | K | I | - | H | Z |

| tzadi | péh | ayin | sammeç | nun | mem |
|-------|-----|------|--------|-----|-----|
| - | Π | O | Ξ | N | M |
| - | P | O | - | N | M |

| | | tav | shin | resh | quf |
|---|---|-----|------|------|-----|
| | | T | Σ | P | Θ |
| | | T | S | R | Q |

Fig. 4   The Old Hebrew alphabet of the mid-ninth century BCE – the same in all but name as the Phoenician alphabet adopted by the Greeks a century earlier (after Yardeni, *Sefer Hactav Ha'ivri [The Book of the Hebrew Script]*, p.16).   Read right to left, as per the direction of writing.

However, we should remember the historical context of the Sanhedrin's decision: as the official imperial language and the lingua franca of most of the Middle East for nearly five hundred years, Aramaic was the Latin of its time in this part of the world – with all the prestige and

19

importance that this implies. Furthermore, it could be argued that opting for the Aramaic script did not amount to a complete renunciation of the Old Hebrew: although the forms of its letters had changed considerably from their ancestral Canaanite origins, in name and function they were still the same characters. In addition, since no great body of work had been committed to or at least had survived in the old script, there was nothing much to lose in terms of a written cultural heritage. Finally, since Old Hebrew was essentially the same script used by the Phoenicians and all other Canaanites, it could be argued that there was nothing uniquely Judean about it anyway.

To all this I would add yet another argument, for which there is no explicit evidence in the sources but is compelling nonetheless: the Aramaic script was *graphically* simply more practical and better suited to the task of large-scale documentation. With its clear discipline of forms designed around a square template, it was certainly developed with this in mind by generations of Mesopotamian scribes. By contrast, the Old Hebrew alphabet, which had been typically limited to comparatively short texts on stone or clay, had little "rhythm" or consistency, and suffered from poor or ill-defined distinctions between certain letters.

Nevertheless, the topic was clearly a sensitive one, and discussions on the subject kept to a minimum. Early Talmudic debates steered a wide berth around it altogether. The unease was clearly never far from the surface, however, and in the late Talmud, in an outburst suggestive of a conscience racked by guilt, Rabbi Yehudah Hanassi (the compiler of the first half of the Talmud and one of its preeminent historical figures) ventured

20

to excuse the abandonment of the old script on the grounds that the Commandments had in fact been given to Moses in the Aramaic script. Given that Moses preceded the birth of the Aramaic script by at least four hundred years, this well-meaning but blatant attempt at rewriting history must have made his colleagues blanch with embarrassment, for his opinion was politely set aside.[3] However, it forced the topic out into the open, and to settle the matter it was decided to adopt the suggestion of an earlier scholar (Rabbi Hisda), namely, that the Old Hebrew script is in fact *ctav libonaah*. The meaning of *libonaah* is a mystery: it isn't Hebrew – its spelling doesn't even comply with Hebrew grammar – but it sounds vaguely pejorative (the Hebrew word *honaah*, for example, means "deception"), and it's possible they deliberately used a Babylonian code word that future generations wouldn't understand. At any rate, the way it was interpreted in the final resolution was that it belonged to the common, i.e., non-Jewish, inhabitants of the land:

> Originally the Torah was given to Israel in the Hebrew script and in the sacred language [Hebrew]; in the time of Ezra the Torah was given in the Assyrian [Aramaic] script and the Aramaic language. They selected for Israel the Assyrian script and the Hebrew language, leaving the Hebrew script and the Aramaic language for the ordinary people. [4]

The irony is that not long after this fateful decision, the Judean leadership was found to have backed the wrong horse. Within a few decades of its selection as the official script of the Hebrew Bible, of the Talmud, and virtually of all subsequent Jewish and Hebrew literature – Aramaic vanished everywhere but in Judea as the preferred language and script of

21

written record. The entire region was conquered by Alexander the Great, and Greek took over as the new language and script of imperial administration for the entire Near East until well into Roman times.

Might the Judeans have changed horses at this point and switched to the Greek script instead? Hardly. Although the Greek alphabet, too, was a descendant of the old Canaanite alphabet and suitable for long texts, Greek culture was entirely alien to Judea and its history. The script had also changed too much since its inception: the function of key characters had changed, others had been dropped altogether, still others had been added, and of course their names had been Hellenized and their forms mirrored as part of the switch of direction to left-to-right. As a result, of all the peoples of the region, only the Judeans and Nabateans (whose version would eventually evolve to become the classical Arabic script) continued to use the Aramaic script.

And so it came to pass that the original Hebrew script was "kicked upstairs" to largely ceremonial roles, such as depicting the name of God in biblical scrolls, coin inscriptions invoking the heroic Israelite kingdoms of old, and so on. In a revival of this practice, some of the coins of modern Israel also boast a word or two in the old script on the back (Fig. 5-a). But today, even educated Israelis cannot read it, nor, oddly enough, are they at all curious as to what it says. The letters on the modern sheqel coin, for example, spell "YHD," i.e., *Yehud* (the old Persian imperial name for Judea), yet most Israelis have no idea what it says; if pressed, they assume it says *sheqel*.

None of this is taught, or even hinted at, in modern Israeli education. Like my friends and everyone else I know, I too assumed, until researching for this book, that the Old Hebrew alphabet was simply an earlier incarnation of the familiar forms of Square Hebrew. Only occasionally did I puzzle at the absence of any intermediate stages to explain the dramatic differences in some cases, or indeed why older texts were sometimes more recognizable than texts from later periods.

a                                        b

Fig. 5    Some modern Israeli coins (a) have revived the practice of Judean admin-
istrations of as late as the second century CE (b) of using Old Hebrew for
symbolic occasions such as coin inscriptions (Courtesy of J. Naveh).

It is a measure both of the historic sensitivity of the subject and of the recent greater security in the nation's cultural identity that in the past few years the Old Hebrew script has been tentatively introduced into the Israeli school curriculum, albeit still in a very limited and somewhat gim-micky fashion ("At the camp, the children will learn to write their names in ancient Hebrew and come away with a little scroll," to quote a school-teacher in a radio interview in 1995). Even then, however, nary a whisper is made of its unceremonious dumping in favor of a younger and once-glamorous sister script.

One outcome of all this is that – to the bemusement, no doubt, of those seeking divinity in the Square Hebrew characters – the Greek and Roman alphabets bear a far greater resemblance to the inscriptions of

23

Moses' tablets or of the scribes of King David than does modern Hebrew (Fig. 4). This acute irony has not been lost on some; indeed, in modern times it has been one of the reasons cited by advocates of Romanization of modern Hebrew – the movement for adopting the Roman alphabet outright.[5]

A return to the Old Hebrew alphabet could therefore make life easier for Westerners in learning to read and write the language – but there is little likelihood of this happening. After two and a half millennia, the Square Hebrew alphabet has formed an inseparable weave with the language, and in any event "outranks" its predecessor by around eighteen centuries. In addition, unlike the situation in the sixth century BCE, far too much religious and cultural Hebrew heritage has been invested in the incumbent script for it to be abandoned now in favor of any other – even its predecessor.

However, the good news is no such drastic measure is necessary, as it just so happens that modern Hebrew already has a legitimate and fully accepted form of writing that both looks different from the Square variety and bears a passing if not spooky resemblance to its European counterparts.

It's called the Modern Hebrew Cursive.

◊

## The Modern Hebrew Cursive

### A new form of Hebrew

The Modern Hebrew Cursive (*ctav rahut moderni*, to give its official Hebrew name) is a form originally developed for quick handwriting and for secular purposes – i.e., for purposes other than writing Holy Scripture. In recent years, in modern Israel, its role has widened, and it is steadily gaining ground as an alternative to the traditional Square script in various printed contexts or as a light, informal counterpoint to it.

As it turns out, adopting this form for one's introduction to the Hebrew script makes it far more accessible to the Western reader.

While most HFL teachers have yet to catch on to this, graphic artists in Israel have seized on the possibilities of the modern cursive with gusto. The results can be seen throughout the Israeli commercial sector, where it is exploited for its intrinsically greater graphic versatility (as we shall see later in Part III), and for its convenient scope in making localized versions of foreign logos that closely mirror their Roman script originals (Fig. 6).

### To link or not to link

Common ancestry and fashionable modern Israeli graphics notwithstanding, it still seems to be a leap of faith to conclude that Hebrew writing can be taught on the basis of any family resemblance between Modern Hebrew Cursive and Roman italics. At best it might be said to be of limited benefit, since it appears to restrict the student within these apparently narrow stylistic boundaries of the two scripts.

Fig. 6   This proposal for a logo for a restaurant is a typical example of the increasing role played by the forms of the Modern Hebrew Cursive in modern Israel as a legitimate alternative to the traditional Square letters (Courtesy of Qualum Graphic Design).

More to the point, there is little evidence of any causal link. Indeed, from the examples of handwriting that have survived, the most we can say is that the Hebrew cursives were influenced by their respective gentile environments of the period. Compare, for example, the strong Arabic influence in fourteenth-century Sephardi (Spanish) Hebrew cursive (Fig. 7) with the distinctly Gothic character of the German Hebrew "semi-cursive" of the same period (Fig. 8).

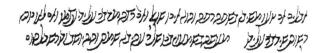

Fig. 7   Spanish Hebrew cursive of ca.1330 CE (MS. Mich. 496. Courtesy of the Bodleian Library, University of Oxford)

26

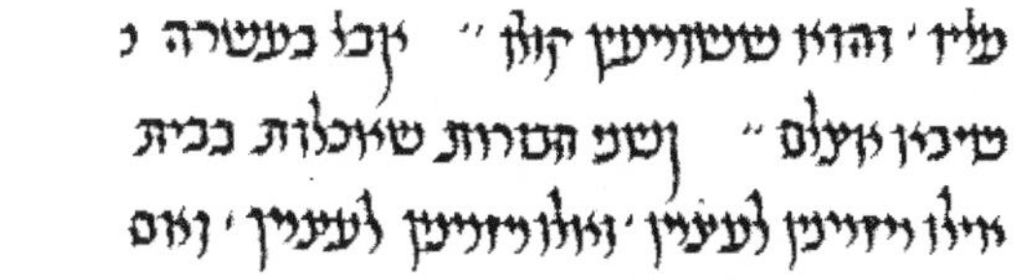

עלֵיז · וֹהֵיו שׁטוֹעֵן קוֹן ″   יָבוֹ בַּעֵשׂרה ג
טֵיבוּן עְוֹעלֵֿם ″   ושֵׁע הַטוֹרֹת שׁוֹכֹלֹוֹת בֵּבֹית
הֵיבוֹ רֵיוֹעֵן לַעֵיִין · וֹהֹיוֹ רֵיוֹעֵן לַעֵיִין · וֹאֹם

Fig. 8   Ashkenazic (German-Jewish) Hebrew "semi-cursive," 1347 (MS. Opp. 339, folio 4 verso. Courtesy of the Bodleian Library, University of Oxford)

The following example of Italian Hebrew cursive of ca. 1520, in its spacing and use of projecting letters, is a close echo of its compatriot Roman script handwriting of the period (Fig. 9).

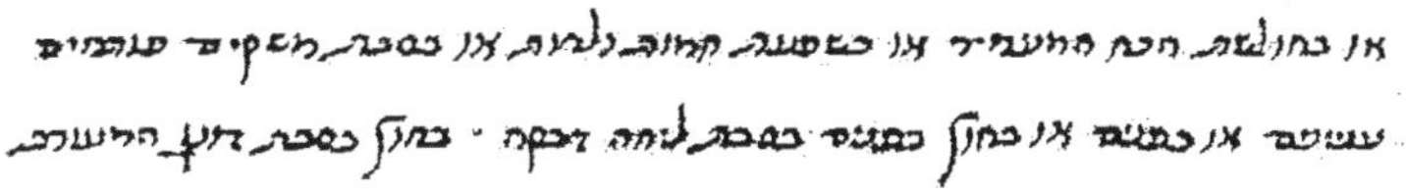

Fig. 9   Italian Hebrew cursive of the sixteenth century (MS. Mich. 536, folio 71 verso. Courtesy of the Bodleian Library, University of Oxford)

## The case against

There are other objections. To begin with, there is genealogical implausibility: Roman lowercase italics and Modern Hebrew Cursive are comparatively recent and entirely independent developments, only very indirectly related in the family tree of Western writing (Fig. 10). When the Old Hebrew script was renounced in favor of the Aramaic (Fig. 10-A), the new "Hebrew script" diverged dramatically from its European cousins (Fig. 10-B). A dramatic narrowing of the gap occurred with the birth of Roman italics and the Modern Hebrew Cursive (Fig. 10-C-D), providing for a shorter and easier bridge between the two scripts than the route offered by conventional methods, which merely "parachute" the

27

student onto modern Square print forms, as if they were entirely unrelated (Fig. 10-E-F). However, this is entirely fortuitous, inasmuch as there was no direct causal connection between the two.

How, then, can there be said to be any evolutionary connection? Particularly as such similarities as do exist between them tend to be where both forms are *different* from the classic printed forms of their respective scripts (Fig. 11).

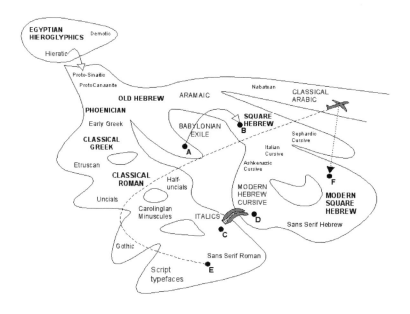

Fig. 10  A schematic "map" of Western writing, with proximity indicating formal similarities between the various alphabets

Then there is the technical argument. The Roman lowercase, as we know it today, is the product of the "Carolingian minuscules" – a form expressly commissioned and implemented by Charlemagne in the ninth

28

century throughout the Holy Roman Empire, in a bid to standardize the regional styles of European calligraphy that were diverging alarmingly to the point of mutual unintelligibility. By contrast, Hebrew has never developed even the *concept* of upper- and lowercase (a bit of good news for you there). Which means that technically its characters must be regarded as uppercase, and so we are not comparing like with like.

Finally, there is the implausibility of intention – or, if you like, the absence of motive. One might understand if, under the influence of their Christian environment, the European Hebrew cursive forms edged toward their Roman equivalents, but more often than not, in the move to lowercase and to italics, it was the *Roman* letter which became more like its Hebrew counterpart rather than the other way around. Since we can safely assume that neither Charlemagne's designers nor Aldus Manutius (the inventor of italics) were striving to emulate the Hebrew script, no conscious historical dynamics could have been at play here.

On the face of it, therefore, the case for a direct link between Roman italics and Modern Hebrew Cursive seems decidedly shaky.

Still, the gun smokes.

### Unexplained similarities

Much of the reason for pursuing the links between Hebrew and Roman scripts is based on turning the aforementioned objections on their head. If conscious emulation is not at play here, why, then, does the lowercase Roman *r* look so uncannily like the mirror image of its Hebrew cousin *resh* – particularly when its parent, the capital *R*, bears no such

29

resemblance? And not just the *r* – but the *l*, *q*, *m*, *z*, too, and, to a lesser extent, the *a*, *g*, *i*, and *t* (Fig. 11).

All these resemble their Hebrew counterparts far more closely than their uppercase forms do. That is already nine of the twenty-two letters of the Hebrew alphabet, which rules out coincidence – and we haven't begun to examine the similarities that *are* accidental.

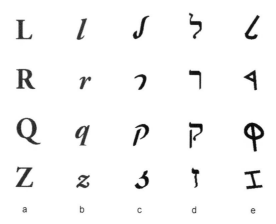

Fig. 11  Examples of letters whose Roman lowercase italics (b) and Modern Hebrew Cursive forms (c) demonstrate a similarity that is not evident between the original Roman (a) and Square Hebrew forms (d), nor necessarily explained by the common Canaanite ancestor (e).

One might suspect that these likenesses are due to a return – conscious or otherwise – to the ancestral, Canaanite form. When distant cousins look alike, one looks at their common ancestor. But closer examination appears to rule this out, since in almost all cases both Hebrew and Roman characters differ from their Phoenician/Old Hebrew forms as much as from their classical incarnations (Fig. 11).

Furthermore, there are examples of letters which bear a striking similarity despite having no historical relationship whatsoever. The classic instance is that of the Roman *c* and the Hebrew *caf.*

The *caf*'s true counterpart is *k*, which in fact is very faithful to their common Canaanite ancestor, being much the same, only upside down (Fig. 12). *C*, on the other hand, is an Etruscan invention, adopted by the Romans to replace the form of the Greek letter *gamma* which they didn't like. This subsequently lost its *g* sound because they had a peculiar difficulty distinguishing between hard *g* and hard *c* (an echo of which we see to this day in Italian words such as *gatto* = cat). Meanwhile, under its Aramaic custodians, the Old Hebrew *kaph* mutated beyond recognition.

The end result of these entirely independent processes is a mirror similarity so compelling that the eye positively rebels against the use of any other letters during transliteration, particularly in common names and words (Fig. 12).

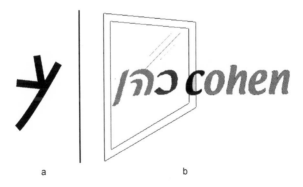

a                    b

Fig. 12 Historically, the true counterpart of the Old Hebrew/Phoenician *caf* (*a*) is the Roman *k*, but the similarity between the Square Hebrew *caf* and the Roman *c* (*b*) is so compelling that traditional transliterations opt for the latter, in defiance of historical accuracy.

31

Another curious resemblance is that between the Roman *F* (upper- or lowercase) and the *F*-sounding version of the Hebrew *p* known as *péh sophit*, as we shall see later. While this is not as striking as the resemblance between the *c* and *caf*, it is significant and extends to all versions of the two characters in the two scripts, including lowercase italics and the Hebrew cursive.

◊

## Chirodynamics

The phenomenon of separate entities, once linked but now independent, developing along the same lines through no apparent causal connection between them, is unintuitive at first but by no means unique.

In physics, applications are now being developed to capitalize on the spooky phenomenon of *entanglement*, whereby two subatomic particles that are part of the same system and then separated remain linked in such a way that any action on one is instantaneously reflected in the other, even if they are separated by immense distances.

Life scientists are well familiar with instances of *evolutionary convergence*, whereby life forms that are only distantly related, or not at all, independently develop similar characteristics in response to the same environmental conditions. Examples of this abound, ranging from the dorsal fins of dolphins and sharks, to the "camera-type" eyes of squid and fish, and to the snouts of South American vs. Australian anteaters.

However, we needn't stretch to analogies in biology or physics. Closer to home, the linguistic theory of *universal grammar*, first put forward by Noam Chomsky in connection with spoken language, suggests that certain hardwired constructions in the human brain allow even young children the world over to form grammatically correct sentences in their mother tongue without resorting to imitation.

Might it be possible, in similar fashion, that the similarities between Roman and Hebrew cursives are due to an innate universal handwriting mechanism that causes latent features of disparate scripts to rise to the surface, even when they are not apparent in the common ancestor?

The answer appears to be yes. Close study of the patterns of writing in both scripts suggests that just such a mechanism exists. Although not as mystifying as quantum entanglement, nor as uncanny as human language structures in the brain, it is nonetheless very real. Simply put, it is a set of natural inclinations of the (right) hand when writing on paper or parchment (as opposed to chiseling, for example, or making indentations in soft clay, as was the practice in antiquity). For the sake of convenience, we might refer to these inclinations collectively as **chirodynamics** (from the Greek *chiro,* meaning "hand").

## The Six Rules

There appear to be six basic rules governing this area. They may be indicative of something more profound, but in essence it comes down to a simple disinclination of the (right) hand to cramp or overextend itself as it writes. Some are less self-evident than others, but all are surprisingly mundane and easily verifiable by yourself:

1. Handwriting tends to lean to the right – irrespective of the direction of writing.

2. When the direction of writing opposes its slant, "barbed hooks" tend to loop.

3. The circular or semicircular elements of all characters (where applicable) are constructed on a common "chirodynamic ellipse," their starting point lying always somewhere between ten and four o'clock (typically at even-hour increments: ten, twelve, two, four, and six).

4. Full circles always start at or near twelve o'clock, and move away from the writing hand (i.e., counterclockwise for right-handers); circles drawn toward the writing hand tend to spiral.

5. Rainbow arcs (i.e., that start and end at the baseline) are tolerated only when writing hand, direction of writing, and slant are all in agreement.

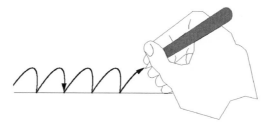

6. Horizontal strokes are tolerated only when drawn in the direction of the writing hand.

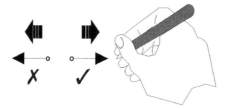

With these principles in mind, we are well placed to understand and implement the transition from the Roman cursive to its Hebrew counterpart.

# Part II

*The Three Steps*

## Step 1: Mirror Writing

We start with a bold premise: *Cursive Hebrew is essentially lowercase Roman letters written in reverse.*

Of course, it's not quite as simple as that – any more than *cat*, *sat*, and *mat* sum up the principles of English spelling. However, just as English-speaking children are typically introduced to such words when learning to read and write, it's a good place to start. Michelangelo once said of his sculptures that they already existed in the raw blocks of marble brought into his studio, and he merely liberated them from their solid confines. In a similar manner, we need only chip away from the reverse forms of Roman characters to liberate the Hebrew form that often lies within. Our chisels, if you will, lie in a series of appropriate qualifications, both cultural and chirodynamic (i.e., the way in which the letters want to be formed).

### It's the Roman wot is backwards

The first point to remember is that Hebrew is written in the opposite direction to Roman and Greek.

'Twas not ever thus. For at least a century or two after adopting the script of the Phoenicians (some time in the tenth or ninth century BCE) the preclassical Greeks generally respected the Canaanite method of writing from right to left (Fig. 13).

ᚈᚑᚷᚷᛒᚠᛈᛗᚾᚩᚻᛗᛁᛜᛟᚻᛁᛄᚴᚦᛜ

Fig. 13 The ancient Greek alphabet, from an inscription dating from the seventh century BCE. Note the right-to-left orientation, just as in Hebrew and Phoenician.

However, they were also prone to slip into a boustrophedon mode of writing – "the way an ox-drawn plow moves." This meant writing one line right to left, the next left to right, and so on (Fig. 14-b). This was a throwback to a previous era, when the original Greek script – a pictographic system developed in Crete around 2000 BCE – had been written that way. Although that script had fallen out of use following the devastation of Crete and mainland Greek kingdoms in a series of earthquakes and invasions by Dorian barbarians around 1100 BCE, the boustrophedon habit lived on.[6]

The boustrophedon practice may seem a little odd to us today, but it is a natural inclination in children first learning to write, and at the time was not unusual. It is evident in the script of the Hittites (ancient inhabitants of Turkey and northern Syria of today) and even in some Egyptian hieroglyphics. At some point in the Classical Era (ca. 500 BCE), however, the Greeks decided to stop thinking of their manuscripts as so many plowed fields and opted for a single, consistent direction. For reasons best known to themselves (perhaps to avoid smudging the ink, or as a final, symbolic act of independence from their Canaanite heritage), they chose this direction to be left-to-right.

40

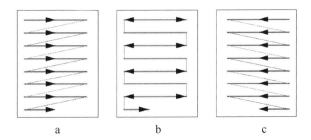

Fig. 14  Unlike the right-to-left direction of Phoenician, Hebrew, and other Canaanite scripts (c) and the left-to-right orientation of later Greek writing (a),
early Greek writing (b) often alternated direction from one line to the next.

And the rest, as they say, is ηιστορια.


## The power of reflection

On the face of it, committing to a reversed direction of writing may seem of little consequence, but its impact is profound, both visually and chirodynamically.

To demonstrate the visual effect, try the following simple experiment with a suitable word – say, *Israel* – to wit:

1.  Write it in all lowercase italics – then flip it, horizontally.

2.  Drop the *e* (for reasons which I will explain presently).

3.  Adjust the slant from left-leaning to right-leaning to match the original (Fig. 15).

41

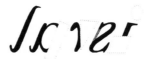

Fig. 15 The word *israel* (*e* omitted) flipped horizontally, then tilted to the right

Note how fragile familiarity can be. Apart from mirroring the image and slanting it differently, we haven't tampered with the actual forms of the letters, yet already we strain to recognize them as Roman characters.

Conversely, show it to a native Hebrew reader and you may well see the first glimmers of recognition – for with a few relatively minor changes (closing a loop at the top of the *s*, blanking out parts of the *a*, *r*, and *i*), we actually reach a fair approximation of the same word in Modern Hebrew Cursive (Fig. 16).

Fig. 16 The same word, with parts omitted and the top loop of the *s* closed

This tells us two things. First, that the psychological impact of a simple mirror reflection is extraordinarily powerful – particularly when disguised by adjusting or removing the original slant. Indeed, it is so potent that Leonardo da Vinci found that it was all he needed to do to render his private writings utterly unintelligible to unwanted onlookers of his day.

The second thing it suggests is that much of the "foreignness" of Hebrew may be ascribed to such relatively superficial external characteristics that can easily be reversed.

Of course, not all examples will be as simple as the one above: were we to use capital letters in the Roman version, for example, or Square letters in the Hebrew, the mirror similarity would largely disappear. The word *Israel* itself is also a little exceptional in that it comprises characters whose graphic similarity in the two scripts has somehow survived – or, to be more precise, was reborn – in the parallel evolution of these two separate branches of the family of writing (Fig. 10).

Nevertheless, you couldn't pull off this trick between two truly unrelated scripts – such as Roman and, say, Chinese or Korean. Nor is the *Israel* example unique: we can repeat the feat equally well with many other words (the *Carmel* logo – of Israeli exported fruit and vegetables – was the standard example I used with my first students). What is more, the symmetry is entirely genuine, inasmuch as the matching letters in these instances are, for the most part, the true historical counterparts of one another, i.e., descended from the same characters of the original Canaanite alphabet.

The fact that we cannot demonstrate the mirror similarity in all or even most cases may confirm the sceptic in rejecting the kinship approach to teaching Hebrew as a nonstarter. But to do so would be like brushing aside the Rosetta Stone on the grounds that it doesn't qualify as a *Dummies* guide to Egyptian hieroglyphics. Of course mastering the Hebrew script is not just a matter of writing Roman in reverse. If it were, there would be nothing to it, and – prejudice or no – the principle would have long since become a cornerstone of instruction in the subject.

However, it is definitely easier than having to learn it from scratch as

43

if it were entirely unrelated. Like a restorer of an Old Master painting, we must peel away the layers of time and stylistic fashion, take into account the materials used, etc., to reveal the original canvas. The mirror similarity of some characters provides the initial clue; to make the actual transition from Roman to Hebrew, we must next apply the chirodynamic rules mentioned in the previous chapter.

You might want to go over the *Israel* example once more, as in it we find the essence of the Three Step method:

1. Write Roman in lowercase italics – in reverse.
2. Match the slant of normal Roman writing and drop certain vowels (and generally phoneticize).
3. Modify the resulting characters in line with their new chirodynamics and Hebrew's generally more reductionist character.


**Putting into practice**

In keeping with all the above, we start by writing English backwards – and in lowercase only. We shall refer to this mode as **Mirror Roman**, or **M.R.** for short (Fig. 17).

Although simple in principle, the practice takes some getting used to, due both to the novelty of writing from right to left, and to the initial weirdness of the letters and words in mirror form. Unless you have had prior experience doing this, the result, when viewed in the mirror or held up to the light back to front, will most likely remind you of your first attempts at writing as a child (Fig. 17).[*]

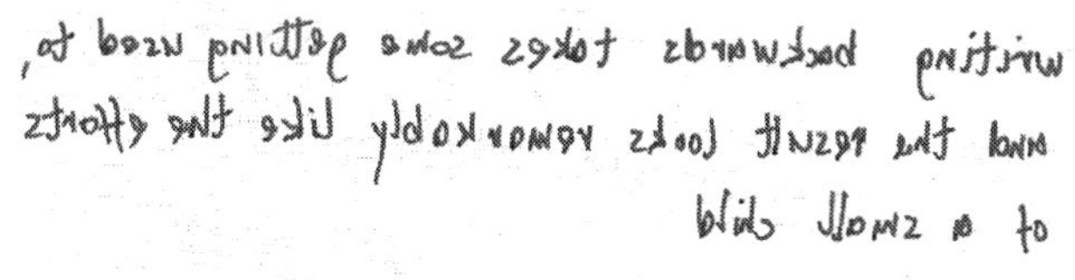

*writing backwards takes some getting used to, and the result looks remarkably like the efforts of a small child*

Fig. 17    A typical first attempt at writing Mirror Roman

By way of comparison, now write the same text in the normal way and hold it up to the mirror or view it from behind against the light.

Once again, if you have never tried this before, you may be surprised how different it looks. What is more, unless your writing is exceptionally clear, chances are you will find it virtually illegible as well. Even today, I never cease to be startled by the strangeness of my own writing when viewed this way (Fig. 18).

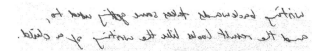

Fig. 18  The mirror image of one's normal handwriting can look startlingly unfamiliar, and almost illegible.

Writing Mirror Roman is good for a laugh, but it also serves a serious purpose. Our basic premise notwithstanding, it illustrates what your Hebrew handwriting will definitely *not* look like. This is for a number of reasons:

---

\*    In fact, it's an old copywriter trick to simulate childish writing in advertisements.

45

*1.  Slant*

You might think that if Roman script writing tends to lean to the right, it follows that in Hebrew it should lean to the left. But you would be wrong: in fact, as predicted in the First Rule of Chirodynamics, the typical Hebrew cursive has precisely the same tendency to lean toward the right (Fig. 19).

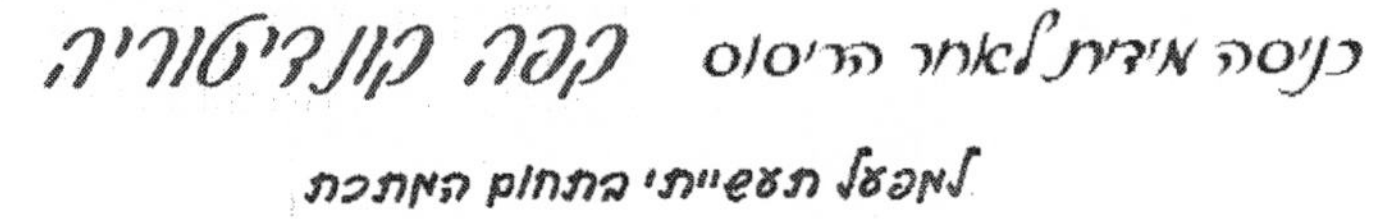

כניסה איזית לאחר היסוד ספר קונדיטוריה
לאפל תעשייתי בתחום האתכת

Fig. 19  Modern commercial typefaces demonstrate the tendency of cursive Hebrew forms to lean to the right, as in European scripts – and not to the left, as a literal interpretation of the mirror idea might suggest. This universality of slant has important consequences.

*2.  Hebrew letters do not join up*

This is a simple outcome of the Second Rule of Chirodynamics. In all likelihood – particularly if you learned American-style penmanship – your normal handwriting displays some degree of joining of letters. In typography, the styles or typefaces where letters are consistently linked to each other are referred to as Scripts (with capital *S*) – as distinct from ordinary *cursive* where the letters are not connected as a rule.

These links – or *ligatures*, in the jargon – are singularly absent in Hebrew, even in its most fanciful modern cursives. This is because Roman and Hebrew occupy opposite sides of the chirodynamic ellipse. Script-like writing is possible in ordinary Roman because its letters typically start at ten, twelve, or two o'clock and sweep down in

46

a counterclockwise curve, bringing the end of the letter to or near the baseline, ready for the next letter. This "*u*-like" method of writing makes it easy to link from one letter to the next (Fig. 20-b, top).

In Hebrew, however, characters are usually built around the precisely opposite arc between the same two points – namely, clockwise from ten o'clock to four o'clock (Fig. 20-b, bottom). We might call this a "*resh*-like" type of writing, after the Hebrew *r* which such an arc represents. As a result, the typical cursive Hebrew character ends at the baseline away from the starting point of the next letter. Any attempt to link between two consecutive letters thus usually entails drawing over the letter just written – in effect crossing it out.

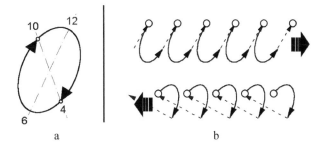

Fig. 20  The Roman cursive has a "*u*-like" character (b, top), while the Hebrew cursive has a reciprocal, "*resh*-like" nature (b, bottom).

This is why Hebrew handwriting can only be cursive in nature – never Script, and yet another reason why your Hebrew writing will never be a simple mirror image of your normal Roman. We can see further illustration of this difference in Hebrew fonts that try to emulate the elegance of Roman Script-like typefaces, and in the handwriting of bilinguals who are equally at home in both scripts (Fig. 21).

Fig. 21 The inherent difficulty in linking up consecutive letters in the Hebrew cursive with baseline ligatures is evident both in commercial fonts designed to emulate Roman Script faces (top) and in the writing of individuals who are equally at home in both scripts (bottom, courtesy of Yael Lotan).

3.   *"The Lady is not for turning"*

The third reason why your Hebrew writing will inevitably differ from the mirror image of your Roman is the fact that the Hebrew script, in all its forms, abhors long pen strokes that loop back on themselves. This is another reason for the non-Script-like character of Hebrew typefaces, and it is not so much an issue of chirodynamics as it is a cultural quirk of the language and the script, both of which lean strongly toward compact expression and minimalism.

**To sum up**

Since Modern Hebrew Cursive (MHC) cannot be classed as a Script style and differs in some of its forms from the Square print variety, the similarities between MHC and the Roman italic style become less mysterious. I should point out, however, that MHC is not technically regarded as the italic form of Square Hebrew, not least because neither the word nor the concept of italics exists at all in Hebrew. True italics modify the form of all or some of the characters in a font set – e.g., italic *a* vs. roman a, *g* vs. g, etc. – but so-called italic forms of Hebrew fonts are merely skewed ("oblique," in the jargon) versions of their standard counterparts (Fig. 22). In time, this may change: secular Hebrew typography is still very much a new art, and since it has had far fewer practitioners, and Jewish concern has traditionally focused on the religious content of Hebrew writing rather than on the design of its characters, it has yet to develop the pedigree, breadth, or rigor of its Roman script counterpart. Consequently, it has a much looser application of established terms and concepts.

אבגדהוזחטיכךלמ
מנןסעפףצץקרשת

Fig. 22 The so-called italic forms of Square Hebrew typefaces (such as Ariel Italic, here) are in fact not true italics at all, but merely oblique versions of their standard counterparts.

The outcome from all the above is that the action of writing from right to left leads naturally to differences in the mirror image of Roman characters. Without knowing a thing about Hebrew script, if you know that much, you're halfway there. The absence of ligatures is one consequence. Others will become apparent as we examine the impact of other chirodynamic rules on individual characters later.

## When in Rome...

In the summer of 1981, some two weeks into a visit to Oslo, I was enjoying an ice cream in the park with my Norwegian hosts. On finishing it, I wanted another, but I had to order it on my own as my friends were busy with their children. As I approached the vendor, I wondered if I had enough Norwegian to make myself understood and decided to chance it and say the first thing that popped into my head:

"*Kan jeg ha eien til?*"

I expected him to look at me quizzically, but to my amazement, he didn't blink an eye, nodded, handed me another and took my money. (Afterwards, my friends confirmed that I had asked correctly.) Translated literally, what I had said was "*Can I have one toward?*" – which makes no sense in any other language I know – yet somehow in Norwegian it just *sounded* like the right way to ask "*Can I have another one?*"

How the correct phrase had popped into my head I don't know. I must have heard it on one or more occasions and it slipped into my subconscious. But the experience brought home to me how, when learning any new language, figuratively slipping into its shoes and going with what feels or sounds right more often than not allows one to guess the correct choice in many situations even without knowing the official grammar. There is no logical reason why in English, for example, one says "aren't I?" other than the fact that "amn't I?" sounds absurd. In my experience, the same reason lies behind every irregular verb and noun in every language.

Learning a new script is much the same. One "makes good," or makes more comfortable, constructions whose origin may have been circumstantial. By writing Mirror Roman you are in effect replicating, in reverse, the switch in direction of writing made by the ancient Greeks. If you then go with the flow of the new direction and drop or change the elements that don't feel comfortable, you will find yourself most of the way toward writing Hebrew characters.

### What now?

Practice writing Mirror Roman for several sessions before moving on to the next step. Your best material is short, informal, but meaningful pieces that you write for yourself in real life – grocery lists, to-do reminders, etc. – rather than abstract sentences of *The quick brown fox jumped over the lazy dog* variety. However, as an appropriate common test bed and to monitor your progress, try also writing out the first verses of the book of Genesis, chapter 11 (the Tower of Babel story – see preliminary pages of this book, and Fig. 23).

Remember:

- Lowercase only – throughout

- Italics/cursive style: no Script-like joining of letters

Don't worry if some letters tend to form differently from the precise mirror image of their original form – that's the point of the exercise.

51

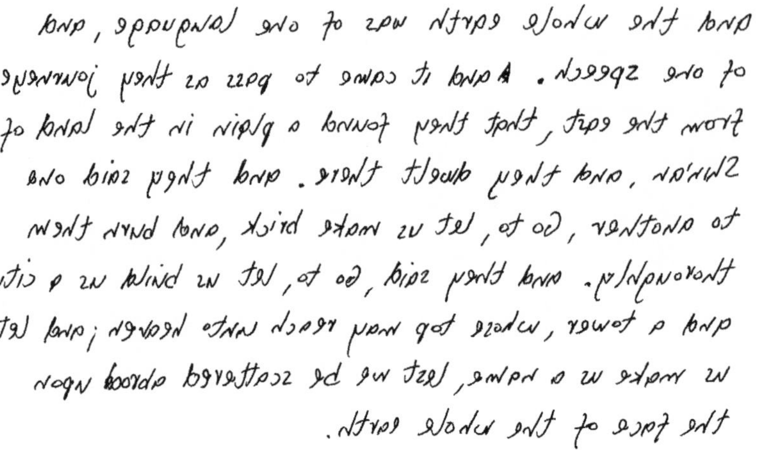

and the whole earth was of one language, and of one speech. And it came to pass, as they journeyed from the east, that they found a plain in the land of Shinar, and they dwelt there. And they said one to another, Go to, let us make brick, and burn them thoroughly. And they said, Go to, let us build us a city and a tower, whose top may reach unto heaven; and let us make us a name, lest we be scattered abroad upon the face of the whole earth.

Fig. 23  Example from the first verses of the book of Genesis, chapter 11, in plain lowercase Mirror Roman

◊

## Step 2: Drop the Vowels

The next step is easy. Having got the hang of writing lowercase Mirror Roman, we now drop certain vowels from the mix.

### Vowel treatment: theory and practice

The Hebrew script, as we said, is reductionist by nature. We saw one example of this earlier, in connection with its dislike of long strokes that loop back on themselves. Another expression of this is in its treatment of vowels. The official line is that Hebrew is an alphabet of consonants only: vowels do not exist as independent letters as they do in the Roman, Greek, and Cyrillic scripts, but only as dots and dashes placed below, above, or to the side of consonants. These dots and dashes are collectively known as **vocalization**, or **pointing** (Fig. 24).

בֵּית־הַכְּנֶסֶת, בֵּית־הַמֶּרְחָץ

Fig. 24 Example of printed Square Hebrew text with vowel sounds indicated by dots and dashes (pointing). These are generally omitted in everyday texts.

Although technically accurate, this explanation creates an impression of a system like certain types of shorthand or SMS texting, *whr wrds r tpclly wrttn wth cnsnnts nly*. Such a scheme is difficult enough in one's own language, so it must be an alarming prospect in one you are still struggling to learn.

53

In practice, however, the complete absence of vowel-letter cues (known in Hebrew as *ctiv Haser* – literally, deficient spelling) is true only of ancient and classical texts. The Phoenicians apparently went for it in a big way, perhaps to leave as much time as possible for the business of trading. It was the norm in Old Hebrew, too – albeit slightly less zealously followed, for reasons which shall presently be clear – and in Aramaic, up to and including the transcription of the Old Testament in the Second Temple period.

Strictly deficient spelling, however, was problematic. As far as we can tell, then as now Hebrew had the five basic vowel sounds (*a, e, i, o, u* – pronounced as in the southern European languages), which meant that the risk of misreading was greater than in other Semitic languages, which typically used only three (*a, i, u*). Indeed, by the start of the Christian era the correct pronunciation of some biblical passages had become a matter of educated guesswork. Fearful that future generations might lose touch altogether with the original pronunciation and meaning of the sacred text, but forbidden by their Talmudic predecessors to add or omit "so much as an iota" to it, rabbinical scholars in the second century CE devised various competing schemes of dots and dashes to represent the correct vowel sounds, one of which ultimately won out and is used to this day.

So far, so hopeful. The bad news is that this pointing scheme is employed today only in biblical texts, in poetry, and in texts for young children or new immigrants. Everywhere else they are omitted (they clutter up the page and are frankly a pain to typeset) – except in words where the intended reading may not be clear from the context. This may sound daunting, but you really do learn fairly quickly to recognize most words and names without *niqud*, as pointing is known in Hebrew. (Honest.)

### Full spelling

Nevertheless, to minimize the difficulties that might arise from unpointed text, recent decades have seen the rise of what is known as *ctiv malé* (full spelling) in most everyday texts – newspapers, books, signs, etc. This makes up to a large extent for the absence of dots and dashes by designating certain letters – specifically, *aleph*, *vav*, and *yod* – to signal the presence of the vowel sounds *a*, *o* or *u*, and *i*, respectively, where these are not obvious from the context or conjugation, e.g., in foreign terms. While these are not real vowel characters in the European sense of the word, in many cases it adds up to much the same thing.

To simulate this full-spelling treatment in Mirror Roman, you should therefore *keep* the vowel characters in all the following instances:

- Whenever a word or syllable starts with a vowel sound
- Most instances of *o* or *u* (pron. *oo*)
- Most instances of *i* (as in *pizza*)
- All diphthongs, e.g., *ai* or *ay*, *aï*, *ou* (as in *mouth*), etc., or consecutive vowel sounds, like *ae* in *maestro*

The upshot of all this is that the only vowels that tend *not* to be explicitly indicated in *ctiv malé* are instances of (short) *a* and *e* sounds in the middle of words. With native Hebrew words, as we said, the pronunciation is usually clear from its conjugation (if it's a verb) or its context. It

55

gets a little trickier with foreign names and words, where of course the rules of Hebrew grammar don't apply. In such cases, an *aleph* is often used to indicate an *a* sound, e.g., in the word *safari*.

### Summary of vowel treatment

We shall learn to recognize and write these "vowel indicator" letters in the next chapter. For now, the point of all the above is to make a number of changes in the vowel treatment of our Mirror Roman in preparation for the third and final step, that of modifications to the M.R. characters themselves. These are:

- Phoneticize. Hebrew, you'll be glad to know, is spelled the way it sounds and even avoids double letters to denote a stressed consonant (instead, a dot is placed in the center of the relevant character – when pointing is used).

- Drop all instances of short *a* and *e* in the middle of words – except where they form consecutive vowels (in which case, drop the *e* only).

- Tack on an *h* to words ending in *ah* or *eh;* this provides the necessary cue that those sounds are present.

- Turn all *y*'s into *i*.

- Turn all sounds of long *a* (as in *day, paint*) and long *i* (*find*) into a double *i* (I'll explain later).

We could apply these rules to the passage we used earlier from the book of Genesis, but rather than deliberately misspell an English text, try transliterating the actual Hebrew of the same verses. In standard Roman lowercase, the words would go as follows (apostrophes separate discrete sounds):

*vaihi col ha'aretz safah ehat, udvarim ahadim.*

*vaihi benos'am miqedem, va'imtze'u biq'ah be'eretz shin'ar – va'ieshvu bah.*

*va'iomru ish el re'ehu: havah nilbenah levenim, venisrefah lisrefah.*

*vat'hi lahem halvena le'aven, vehaheimar haiah lahem lahomer.*

*vaiomru: havah nivneh ir umigdal verosho bashamiim, vena'aseh lanu shem, pen nafutz al pnei col ha'aretz.*

Once the vowels are dropped in accordance with the aforementioned rules, the result in Mirror Roman looks something like Fig. 25.

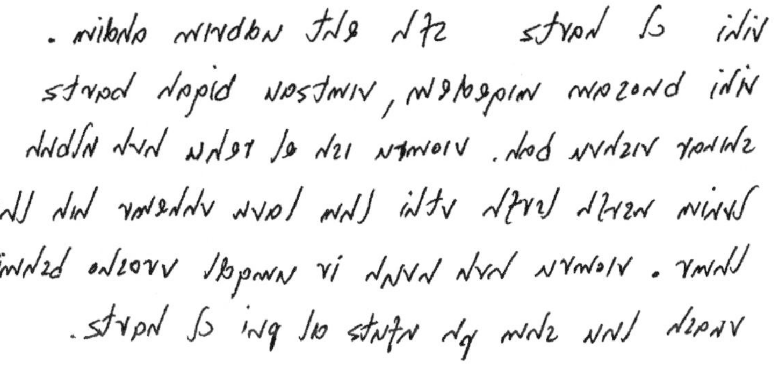

Fig. 25 The Hebrew of the first verses of the book of Genesis, chapter 11, transliterated in Mirror Roman after Hebrew-like vowel treatment

(Since biblical Hebrew employs fairly deficient spelling, applying the rules we listed earlier results in the addition of two or three vowel indicators that aren't there in the original, but we'll let that go.)

**Final word**

This is an important stage. By writing transliterated Hebrew in this way you are detaching your mind from the notion of writing English, thereby conditioning it psychologically for the new script. You are also absorbing subtle but important cues about the structure of Hebrew words, its treatment of vowels, etc., which will stand you in good stead if and when you go on to study the language itself. Finally, you are giving your hand and brain valuable practice in the physical activity of writing from right to left.

If you like, try your hand at the additional examples of transliterated Hebrew provided in the appendix – particularly the familiar terms of foreign origin. However, you can just as effectively carry it out on bits of English from your ordinary routine.

◊

## Step 3: Simplify and Make Comfortable

This is the brass tacks – the stage where we get properly acquainted with the Hebrew characters for the first time and learn to write the real thing, instead of Mirror Roman caricatures. It is also the biggest of the Three Steps, of course, because each of the letters has to be dealt with in turn. Individually, however, the jump in most cases is modest, if not trivial.

### From ugly duckling...

As you practiced Mirror Roman, you may have felt a rhythm beginning to build into your writing, making it faster and more confident.

Beyond a certain point, however, you perhaps noted that it refuses to get any easier. It's as if something is preventing you from reaching the "higher gears" of fluency and ease, as in your normal writing. Moreover, the effect is not uniform across the alphabet. Some characters (such as *c*, *i*, and *o*) feel immediately comfortable in their mirror form, others (*v*, *w*, *x*) feel and look much the same by virtue of their symmetry, while still others (*q*, *z*, *t*) seem almost comfortable but need just a little tweaking before they can truly "settle in." The rest seem to require more fundamental changes (Fig. 26).

*p s t   x w v   o i ɔ*

Fig. 26 With practice, Mirror Roman writing becomes more confident, but the new direction is not uniformly comfortable across the alphabet.

The varying degrees of comfort you feel are all symptomatic of the chirodynamics we discussed in Part I and are due to the extent to which the characters in question still comply with the six basic rules after mirroring. In most instances, resolving these discrepancies will transform the character in question into its Hebrew equivalent, where such exists.

## Overview

Specifically, we find that characters that feel immediately comfortable in their mirror form (*c*, *i*, and *o*) appear in Hebrew with little or no change – although, because Hebrew treats vowels differently and is generally more reductionist, they don't necessarily mean the same thing. A more reliable transformation (i.e., where the Mirror Roman form *is* the equivalent Hebrew consonant) occurs in consonants that settle down after minor modifications (e.g., *f*, *q*, *t*, *z*). Meanwhile, letters such as *u*, *w* and *x*, which exploit their symmetry to avoid changing at all, are conveniently dropped from the line-up altogether, as they are found to have no Hebrew counterparts anyway.

That is the situation in principle. We can now proceed to discussing the changes in each individual letter through the action of writing.

60

Because certain themes emerge in their attributes, we will examine the letters not in alphabetical order, but in groups according to their chirodynamic behavior. We start with the Hebrew *resh*, as it represents the most fundamental attributes of the alphabet as a whole. We might refer to these groupings as follows:

- **Whalers:** Characters featuring "harpoon hooks" that tend to go loopy in their mirror form and must be modified accordingly

- **Clockwise Rebels:** Characters whose circular or semicircular elements resist being drawn in true mirror fashion and must therefore be executed differently

- **Kissing Cousins:** Characters whose Mirror Roman forms are, with relatively minor changes, resolved to match their Hebrew counterparts

- **Happy Accidents:** Characters whose Mirror Roman forms bear a striking resemblance to their Hebrew counterparts by virtue of "evolutionary convergence"

- **Wallflowers:** Characters that have no partner whatsoever in the other camp.

Between these groupings we shall cover the entire ground of both Roman and Hebrew alphabets. Our point of departure in each case, as we said, is the lowercase italic form of the Roman characters. You should practice each Hebrew letter as we go along on a separate sheet of paper (on its own, to get the feel of it; don't feel obliged to copy the word examples shown until you feel you recognize the other letters being used and are confident enough to try them out together). To get you in the habit of reading from right to left, illustrations are henceforth laid out in that fashion when referring to Mirror Roman or Hebrew writing.

Pronunciation note: in the names of all Hebrew characters the emphasis is on the first syllable.

## Whalers (*b, h, m, n, p, r*)

*r*

> *"When the direction of writing opposes its slant, 'barbed hooks'*
> *tend to loop." (*Second Rule of Chirodynamics*)*

The move from Mirror Roman *r* to Hebrew *resh* helps illustrate a fundamental problem with all letters that use a "barbed tip" or "harpoon hook" between the downstroke and the arch. We refer to these collectively as *whalers* – due to this harpoon analogy, and because they happen to be the consonants of the mnemonic *harpoon mob*. As the simplest of the six, the solution for the letter *r* is representative of the treatment for the others in the group (Fig. 27).

Fig. 27  Whaler letters of normal Roman share a harpoon-hook-like transition between the downstroke and the arch. This is awkward in right-to-left writing, so alternatives must be found.

62

What we find is that this barbed tip comes naturally and easily when the direction and slant of writing are in agreement (e.g., both to the right), but not otherwise. In normal Roman, the first downstroke (technically known as the *ascender, descender,* or *stem,* depending on its direction and height) introduces a necessary breather and rhythm into the formation of these characters – which is why it was invented in the first place. In Mirror Roman, however, which still slants to the right but proceeds to the left, not only is the hook not helpful, it fights against the flow and tends irresistibly to become a loop (Fig. 28-a-b). Try it and see for yourself.

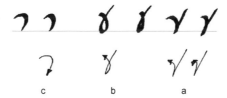

c          b          a

Fig. 28  The tendency of the harpoon hook of the *r* (a) to turn into a loop in its mirror form (b) can be resolved by dropping the stem altogether, leaving just the curved stroke clockwise from ten o'clock (c). This precisely corresponds to the Hebrew *resh*.

Coincidentally, the result does correspond to a Hebrew character – the *ayin*, of which more later – but it gets in the way of writing the Mirror Roman versions of the aforementioned characters. (If you noticed this problem, you now know why.)

In the case of the *r*, the solution is to drop the stem altogether and draw the curved stroke only. Since the hand dislikes drawing right-to-left rainbow arcs (Fifth Rule of Chirodynamics), this is done in a simple arc, from ten to four o'clock, in an action familiar to us from the arc of a standard lowercase *n* or *h* (Fig. 28-c). We shall call this the *resh*-stroke – and mark it well, for it is the most fundamental building block of Hebrew cursive and recurs in several other characters.

*b*

You might think the solution to writing a M.R.. *b* is easy: just draw a standard *d*. But that won't do, since the standard *d* is designed to leave you, on its completion, heading toward the next letter on the right (Fig. 29). Besides, as we have said, Hebrew abhors strokes that turn back on themselves.

Fig. 29  The standard *d* is designed to leave you, on its completion, heading toward the next letter on the right – which is awkward when you're writing in the opposite direction.

So we have no choice but to form the *b* in one sweep after all – starting from the top of the ascender. The aforementioned loop tendency, however, leads to an unsatisfactory and inconsistent result (Fig. 30).

Fig. 30        The problem with the Mirror Roman *b*

The solution is similar to that of the *resh*: instead of the straight

64

ascender of the Mirror Roman *b* (Fig. 31-a), make an arc – slightly broader and flatter than the *resh*-stroke – starting from ten o'clock, down to the baseline, followed by a smaller arc underneath it in the opposite direction (Fig. 31-b).

Fig. 31        From Mirror Roman *b* to Modern Hebrew Cursive *bet*

You may note the latter arc is in violation of the Fifth Rule of Chirodynamics – the only instance in Hebrew cursive of an arc drawn right to left from the baseline – but it just about gets away with it by virtue of being small and done "on the rebound." Even so, it is a teentsy bit awkward, and in recent years there has been a strong trend in commercial Hebrew cursive fonts to avoid it by scrapping the textbook version altogether in favor of an early-modern form that looks rather like the figure *2* (Fig. 31-c). This sidesteps the lower arch problem altogether and has a graphic elegance missing in the standard version. However, both in the classroom and in the writing of most people today the official form still predominates, so you are best advised to stick to it. The two may seem hard to reconcile, but when we acquaint ourselves with the Square form in Part III we shall see how they both came about.

The other important fact to note about the *bet* is that it is often *v*-sounding. This is its "soft" form – a feature that repeats itself in five other

65

characters (*gimmel, dalet, caf, péh,* and *tav* – all six known collectively by the Hebrew mnemonic *beged cefet).* The rule is simple: when it starts a word or comes after a closed syllable (i.e., one that ends with a conso-nant), the *bet* is hard (*b*). In all other instances – particularly at the end of words – it is soft (*v*). We can see this in different versions of *bet*-using words which in English transliteration might seem unrelated – e.g., *av* (father) vs. *abba* (dad) – Fig. 32.

*abba*
(dad)

*av*
(father)

Fig. 32  The letter *bet* is sometimes *b*, sometimes *v*, depending on its position in a word.

There is another *v*-sounding letter that can appear in any part of a word and is therefore used where the *bet* cannot be. This is the *vav*, of which more later.

## *h* (1)

> *"Rainbow arcs from the baseline are tolerated only when writ-ing hand, direction, and slant are all in agreement." (*Fifth Rule of Chirodynamics*)*

If the Mirror Roman *h* is not quite as awkward as the *b*, it's only because one can fudge it somewhat as an inverted *v*-like peak, which right-to-left writing does tolerate (Fig. 33-a). Still, the effort tends to make for a scrappy result, so – as with the *r* – the solution is to lose the ascender altogether and focus on forming the arc only.

To avoid the awkwardness of a rainbow arc in the wrong direction, we once again dispense with the ascender, then split what's left into two strokes: a basic *resh*-stroke, followed by (pen off paper!) the left flank drawn downwards from the same starting point (Fig. 33-b). The result is a *Het* (Fig. 33-c) – historical counterpart of the Greek and Roman *h* and namesake of the original Canaanite ancestor. It is not a true aspirated *h*, however, but has a soft guttural quality, like the Spanish *j*.

c         b         a

Fig. 33                 From Mirror Roman *h* to *Het*

## *h* (2)

The simple, aspirated *h* in Hebrew is the letter *héh* (pron. *hay*). Its original form in the Old Hebrew and Phoenician alphabet (Fig. 34-a) was co-opted by the Greeks and Romans to represent the vowel *E*, but in its Aramaic incarnation, and thereafter in Square Hebrew, it somehow became more like a variation of the *Het*.

Consequently, it uses the same *resh*-stroke as the *Het* (Fig. 34-b) and differs only in that the second stroke starts from around halfway down, leaving a gap between the two (as if to allow the air through – Fig. 34-c). To ensure this gap is clear, this second stroke is placed well under the wing of the *resh*-stroke and is often made into a little squiggle, as if echoing the bigger arch in miniature (Fig. 34-d).

Fig. 34                              Making *héh*

## *m*

With not one but two right-to-left rainbow arcs to its name, *m* makes a particularly poor transition to the other side of the looking glass. The result inevitably looks and feels like an unhappy mirrored *n* with an apologetic appendage (Fig. 35-a).

On this occasion, the Modern Hebrew Cursive *mem* appears to keep the stem of its Roman cousin to suggest the first of two crests, with a definite trough between them (Fig. 35-b). Then, in a typically Hebrew-reductionist throwback to its original Egyptian and Canaanite meaning (water), it ends with the next downstroke. Don't worry if the result looks like a reverse lowercase *n* (Fig. 35-c) or an oblique normal uppercase one – we shall cater for that letter separately.

Fig. 35  In common with many characters, the Hebrew *mem* (*c*) is like a simplified, truncated version of its Mirror Roman cousin.

The story doesn't end there, however, as *mem* is also one of five

68

Hebrew letters that assume a different form at the end of a word. Don't ask why just yet (I'll explain in Part III), but in its cursive guise, the *mem sophit* (terminal *mem*, from *sof* = end) looks like a lowercase *p* – except the loop is smaller and elliptical, and the whole letter is designed to be of standard size, i.e., the descender is not expected to go below the baseline (Fig. 36).

Fig. 36  The *mem sophit* – the form *mem* takes on at the end of words – is superficially like a small *p*, except the descender does not, as a rule, go below the baseline.

*n*

With the *n*-like option already nabbed by the *mem*, the Mirror Roman *n* has to be something else altogether, but it's not sure what. And indeed, the Hebrew *nun* (pron. *noon*, only more quickly) has ventured far from its Canaanite origins (Fig. 37-a). Consequently, its Mirror Roman form (Fig. 37-b) is of no use, and it must be learned the old-fashioned way. In its ancient guise the *nun* had a fairly distinct and consistent form very reminiscent of its Greek and Roman form. However, during its Aramaic/Square Hebrew phase the curvy downstroke came to be regarded as the main feature instead, resulting in a *j*-like cursive character that tends to dip below the baseline, quite unlike its European cousin (Fig. 37-c).

Like the *mem*, *nun* also has a special terminal version, which in cursive form is simply a long downstroke that extends well below the baseline (Fig. 37-d).

d          c          b          a

Fig. 37  The Modern Hebrew Cursive *nun* is a small *j*-like character at the beginning and middle of words (c). Its form at the end of words, is a plain, long
downstroke extending well below the baseline (d).


*p*

> *"Full circles always start at or near twelve o'clock and move
> away from the hand (counterclockwise for right-handers); circles
> in the opposite direction tend to spiral." (*Fourth Rule of Chi-
> rodynamics*)*

With its long descender, the barbed hook of the Mirror Roman *p* is
the whaler character most prone to go loopy (Fig. 38-b). But in principle
the Hebrew and Roman letters have had much the same idea in mind
with regard to the original Canaanite *péh* (Fig. 38-a). Square Hebrew,
being modeled on a square template, characteristically interpreted the
curve of the downstroke as a right-angle "pipe-bend," while the Roman *P*,
as we know, made it straight. But both letters set out to close – or nearly
close – the top part of the original Canaanite character.

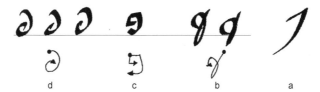

Fig. 38  The Mirror Roman *p* (b) and the Square Hebrew *péh* (c) share the same essential theme: to close – or nearly close – the top part of the ancestral Canaanite *péh* (a). The cursive Hebrew goes the other way, as spirals only come naturally when they are drawn clockwise (d).

True to its mission of providing a more rounded, fluid version of the Square script, the Modern Hebrew Cursive interprets the Square *péh* as a single-stroke circular spiral. However, since counterclockwise spirals are not comfortable, a clockwise spiral is used instead, starting at or near twelve o'clock, effectively turning the Square form upside down (Fig. 38-d).

**Also f**

Incidentally, the *péh* has a soft version, representing the *f* sound. As with the letter *bet*, this occurs everywhere except at the start of words or after a closed syllable (the *beged cefet* rule). Graphically, there is no distinction between the two, other than a notional dot in the center when it is hard (*p*-sounding), which is typically shown only in explicitly pointed texts. This can cause confusion occasionally, but only in words or names of foreign origin, which aren't always considerate enough to observe the rules of Hebrew grammar. Not surprisingly, one of the first things the

71

Greeks did after borrowing this alphabet was to invent a dedicated *f* letter – Φ – to use whenever they pelt – sorry, *felt* – like it.

Finally, like the *mem* and *nun*, the *péh*, too, has a special form at the end of words (don't worry, there are only two more to go), called – you guessed it – *péh sophit*. This is *always f*-sounding (when a hard *p* is required at the end of a word or name – as in *7-Up* or *Forrest Gump* – a regular *péh* is used). It is the one we remarked on earlier as looking a lot like *f*, and we will return to it later in connection with that letter.

## Clockwise Rebels (*a, d, g, o, q*)

### *a*

> *"Full circles always start at or near twelve o'clock and move away from the hand (counterclockwise for right-handers)."*
> (Fourth Rule of Chirodynamics)

The first letter of the Roman alphabet is typical of a group of characters which also includes *d*, *g*, *o*, and *q*. As you know, the normal Roman version of these letters makes a complete counterclockwise circle from two or twelve o'clock before moving on (Fig. 39).

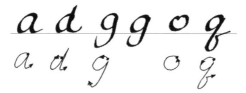

Fig. 39     The clockwise rebels in normal Roman guise

Logic says the Mirror Roman version should do the opposite: i.e., clockwise circles from ten o'clock. But once again, the mirror is overruled by the laws of chirodynamics. As a result, the cursive *a*, that most innocent and common example of normal Roman writing, becomes a surprising nuisance when attempted in reverse. Even if you manage to persuade the hand to do it fluently, it is nearly impossible to get a consistent result – particularly when writing at speed (Fig. 40).

Fig. 40        The Mirror Roman *a* is surprisingly awkward.

(In case you're wondering why, in that case, the ellipse of the *mem sophit* – Fig. 36 – is acceptable, the answer is twofold:

- Because that is not a true circle but an ellipse – a subtle but crucial difference
- Because there it is used exclusively at the end of words, so the downstroke is not expected to lead on to another letter and can therefore anchor it with a simple stroke downwards.)

The strategy here, as with the *Het* earlier, is to break up the character into two separate strokes: a normal *c*-like character (counterclockwise, of course), followed by a straight stroke, representing the stem, to the left side of the *c* – like an American cents symbol (¢) where the straight line is shifted to the left (Fig. 41).

Fig. 41                    Drawing a cursive *aleph*

The result corresponds to the Modern Hebrew Cursive *aleph*.

An acceptable, if less common, alternative is to replace the *c*-like stroke with an arrowhead-like form, like that of a Roman *k*. Unlike the *k*, however, the stem stroke must be drawn second, not first, and it tends to be not as high (Fig. 42).

Fig. 42  The *k*-like version of the MHC *aleph* (a) and its Old Hebrew and Phoenician ancestors (b, c)

While it is not a coincidence that the result is very similar to the original Old Hebrew and Phoenician *aleph* (Fig. 42-b-c), the similarity is not intentional. This is the only example of a Hebrew character that has apparently so forsaken its Square version in favor of its Old Hebrew form, and the reason, as we shall see in Part III, had nothing to do with nostalgia and everything to do with chirodynamics.

**Not just a pretty A**

The final and very important point to make here is that although it was co-opted by the Greeks and Romans to represent the letter *A*, the

74

*aleph* is not and never has been committed exclusively to the *a* vowel.

Vowels in Hebrew are like infants: they cannot venture out alone and must be "carried" – usually by the preceding consonant. In situations where there is no such carrier (as in words starting with a vowel, or in the transition between consecutive vowels, like the aforementioned *ma-estro* or indeed *Isra-el*), the *aleph* steps into the breach to provide support as a silent "vowel carrier." In fact, its versatility in this respect makes it ideal as a placeholder for various vowel sounds, allowing different conjugations of a given root, e.g., *amen* (amen, pron. *ah-men*) and *emunah* (belief).

In modern conventions of *ctiv malé* (full spelling), *i*, *o*, and *u* sounds are often indicated by the addition of other letters, as we shall see later. However, in very common words, often no such indicators are used as the correct vowel is either already known or inferred from the context (Fig. 43).

| *el / al* | *ima* | *im / em* | *amen / oman* |
| (to; a god / don't) | (mom) | (if / mother) | (amen / artist) |

Fig. 43 In its main role as a "vowel carrier," the *aleph* can represent any of the five basic vowels, which in some cases is clear only from the context. Only when transliterating foreign words is it used to indicate the short *a* vowel.

That said, the *aleph* on its own more often carries a short *a* sound than any other vowel – which is why it is often used to indicate that sound in Hebrew transliterations of foreign words and names, as in *safari* (as cited earlier), *jazz*, *Hawaii*, etc.

# *d*

With its full clockwise circle going from ten o'clock instead of twelve and a "turn-back" ascender, Mirror Roman *d* is as awkward as they come (Fig. 44-b). Like the *n*, however, the Hebrew *dalet* (pron. **dah**-*let*) has strayed too far from its ancient ancestor (Fig. 44-a) to have any meaningful link to its European counterparts, and it is best learned the traditional way, i.e., by rote.

When we get to its Square version (p. 114) we will understand how this came about, but the cursive *dalet* – which starts, like so many others, from ten o'clock – is most easily described as a small, truncated *3* (Fig. 44-c).

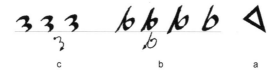

c           b           a

Fig. 44  The problems with Mirror Roman *d* (b) and its solution – the Hebrew cursive *dalet*

The truncation is critical: the bottom of the letter should run smack into the baseline vertically or nearly so, else it might be confused with the cursive letter *tzadi* (Fig. 80).

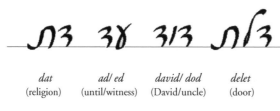

| *dat* | *ad/ ed* | *david/ dod* | *delet* |
|-------|----------|--------------|---------|
| (religion) | (until/witness) | (David/uncle) | (door) |

Fig. 45          Examples of words with *dalet*

# g

As you know, even in normal Roman writing a proper *g* is sometimes difficult when you're in a hurry – particularly when you are trying to link to it in the middle or end of a word. Often one ends up fudging it as a kind of elongated *s* or half a figure *8* (Fig. 46).

Fig. 46          The case of the fudged *g*

It should come as no surprise, therefore, that the Mirror Roman *g* should prove just as tricky.

Interestingly, the mirror image of this fudge looks not too far off the actual Hebrew cursive *gimmel* (Fig. 47).

Fig. 47          The mirror image of the fudged *g*

I should stress, however, that this is only an approximation. You should, in fact, avoid "mirroring the fudge" too literally, as it might be confused with another letter (the *caf sophit* – Fig. 69, p. 94). Instead, remove the source of the problem – the clockwise circular head of the Mirror Roman *g* – and replace it with a simple "forelock" squiggle instead. Then celebrate your new-found freedom with a generous sweeping *c*-shaped arc, giving free rein to its tendency to extend below the baseline (Fig. 48).

*gamal*  *galil*  *gan*  *dag*
(camel)  (Galilee)  (garden)  (fish)

Fig. 48  The price for the *gimmel*'s simplicity is that – unlike its Roman counterpart – it must never be fudged.

Incidentally, the *gimmel* is always a hard *g*: the soft *g*, or *j*, sound is not native to Hebrew.

## o (u, v)

Historically, the Greek and Roman *o* are adaptations of the Phoenician/Old Hebrew character immediately preceding the *péh*, called *ayin* (pron. *eye-een*). The name means "eye" in all Semitic languages, and the character was inspired by the Egyptian hieratic of the same meaning – a simple circle with a dot in the center. Like the *aleph*, the *ayin* is not a vowel but a carrier for orphan vowels. The Greeks and Romans had no patience for such niceties and simply assigned its graphic form exclusively to the *o* vowel, which of course is true to this day. In the meantime, the shape of the Hebrew *ayin* changed beyond recognition under its Aramaic patrons, so much so that the circle was reassigned to another letter – all of which we shall come to later.

78

**As o**

Which still leaves us with the question how the *o* sound is represented in Hebrew. Given Hebrew's different handling of vowels, the answer is not straightforward. The short answer is with a dot – known as a *Holam* – which is placed notionally above rather than below its carriers (Fig. 49). Like other dots and dashes of explicit pointing, the *Holam* is hardly seen in everyday usage, but, you will be glad to know, its presence is often indicated by an *i*-like character known as *vav*.

Unlike the *aleph* or *ayin*, the *vav* cannot initiate the *o* sound on its own at the start of a word or after a closed syllable. When it does carry a vowel, it acts as a *v* (see below). But as an indicator of the *Holam*, it is a classic hallmark of *ctiv malé* (full spelling). When the *vav* is present, the *Holam* dot is placed directly above it – completing the resemblance to the Roman *i* – and is known as *Holam malé* (a full *Holam*). Without it, the *Holam* is supported between the "shoulders" of the consonants on either side and is known as *Holam Haser* (deficient *Holam*). In certain very common words, the *Holam* is always deficient – however full the spelling – as these words are sufficiently recognizable in their own right (Fig. 49).

|   *o*   |   *poh*   |   *boqer*   |   *col*   |   *lo*   |
|---------|-----------|-------------|-----------|----------|
|  (or)   |  (here)   |  (morning)  |  (every)  |  (no)    |

Fig. 49  In very common words, the *o* sound (pron. like *au* in *auto*) is strictly implicit (*lo, col, poh*). In most other cases, however, it can be indicated by the letter *vav*. (The pointing shown is for illustration only, and normally absent.)

You may find it strange at first to visually reconcile the *o* sound with the form that you normally associate with *i*. If it helps, use the trick that I used when I was learning all this, which is to imagine it's a cylinder as seen from two different angles: the Roman letter being the top view, and the Hebrew one its side elevation (Fig. 50).

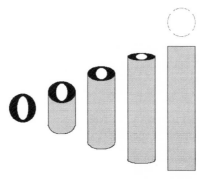

Fig. 50   The transition from *o* to *Holam malé* as different views of a notional cylinder

## As u

Occasionally the vowel sound indicated by the *vav* is not *o*, but *u* (pron. *oo*) – a practice familiar to us from Latin, where *V* represented both *v* and *u*.

The dot in this case (when explicit pointing is used) is placed next to the *vav*'s left midriff, where it is known as a *shuruq malé*. As with the *Holam malé*, the *vav* in this role can only *indicate* the *u* sound, not initiate it. When the *vav* is absent (*shuruq Haser*) the vowel is signaled by three dots on a ten-to-four diagonal (Fig. 51).

| yehoshua | yeshu | yerushaliim | yehudah |
|----------|-------|-------------|---------|
| (Joshua) | (Jesus) | (Jerusalem) | (Judea/Judah) |

Fig. 51 When acting as a *u*-sound indicator, the *vav* has an implicit dot to its left side. However, in certain words and names (e.g., *yehoshua*) the sound itself is strictly implicit and no *vav* is used.

## As v

When it is not busy indicating *o*'s or *u*'s, the *vav* retires with a nice cup of cocoa and does what it likes best, namely, to serve as a simple *v* consonant. In this role, it wears no dot whatsoever on its person. Unlike the soft form of *bet*, it can serve in this capacity anywhere – including at the beginning of a word or after a closed syllable. This is just as well because, as a *v*-sounding prefix, it serves as the standard form of the Hebrew word for "and." It is also used to represent the *v* in foreign words where *bet* couldn't apply (see Fig. 30, p. 64) or would be more ambiguous (Fig. 52).

| vizah | avir | qav | stav | vered | vav |
|-------|------|-----|------|-------|-----|
| (visa) | (air) | (line) | (autumn) | (rose) | (hook) |

Fig. 52 Unlike the soft *bet*, the *vav* can serve as a *v* consonant anywhere.

81

**In all three guises**

All three guises of *vav* may be seen in the Hebraized word *virtuoz* (virtuoso) and in the three possible readings of the combination *d-v-d*, with their respective vowel pointing made explicit (Fig. 53).

| | | | |
|---|---|---|---|
| *virtuoz* | *dood* | *dod* | *david* |
| (virtuoso) | (hot water tank) | (uncle) | (David) |

Fig. 53 The different guises of *vav* – two examples. In practice, the pointing is normally left out, unless the correct reading isn't clear from the context.

## *q*

Back on the firmer ground of proper consonants, here's an easy one for you. The Hebrew *quf* is the opposite number of the Roman *q* and namesake of the original Phoenician and Old Hebrew character (Fig. 54-a), which happily both still resemble. Because of this, the official convention in Israel is now to use a *q* (rather than *k*) to represent *quf* in Roman transliterations of virtually all Hebrew terms that use *quf* – e.g., *Ashqelon*, *Bezeq*, *sheqel* (even – absurdly – *Qeisaria*, a.k.a. "Caesarea"). This of course is at odds with traditional European transliterations, since it disregards the rule that *q* must always be followed by a *u*. The result may therefore look odd, but for our purposes it is useful as it should help you spot when it is used in Hebrew terms and when not.

As with the *a*, the head of a mirror image *q* involves a full clockwise circle. The downstroke helps to anchor this (Fig. 54-b), but not enough

82

to overcome the awkwardness except perhaps when terminating a word. Which, if you think about it, is probably why the normal Roman *p* isn't drawn this way, but rather with the downstroke first, then the loop (Fig. 54-c).

Fig. 54   The Mirror Roman *q* wants to be drawn like a normal *p*, but breaking it into two separate components is more comfortable when writing right to left.

Not surprisingly, the *quf* is also carried out in two strokes, but to suit the right-to-left direction of writing, the order is reversed: first a *resh*-stroke, then the downstroke – but starting well clear, as in the letter *héh* (Fig. 34). The result is essentially a Mirror Roman *q* with gaps (Fig. 55).

Fig. 55          The *quf* represents the resolution of the Mirror Roman *q*.

As we shall see later, *quf* is one of two *k*-sounding letters in the Hebrew alphabet. In theory, it is the more "Semitic" of the two, as it is supposed to be guttural in pronunciation, but among modern Hebrew speakers this distinction has all but died out, and the Academy of the Hebrew Language has decreed that it should represent most *k*-like sounds in foreign words and names, regardless of the letter used in the original (Fig. 56). There are a few specific exceptions to this rule, as we shall see later.

83

| banq | qatoli | qafeh | qilo |
| (bank) | (Catholic) | (coffee) | (kilo) |

Fig. 56 The *quf* is the letter of choice when transliterating *k*-like sounds of foreign (i.e., non-Semitic) words and names, regardless of their original spelling.

## Kissing Cousins (*i, l, s, t, z*)

### *i (y)*

Thanks to its simplicity, the Mirror Roman *i* is, as we have seen, as comfortable in a right-to-left direction as it is in ordinary Roman. Like that other symmetrical form, *o*, the character as it stands doesn't quite correspond to its Hebrew counterpart – but it's not too far off, particularly when you take into account Hebrew's penchant for minimalism.

The Roman *i* is of course fairly simple already, but the *yod* – whose Canaanite ancestor inspired the Greek letter *iota* – goes one better. Think of it as the top half of the lowercase *i*, or an extension of its dot to about halfway down to the baseline (Fig. 57).

c          b          a

Fig. 57 Carrying reductionism to the extreme, the cursive *yod* is like a lowercase *i* that is carried only halfway down to the baseline. The length is critical, to distinguish it from *vav* and terminal *nun*, as demonstrated by the word *yavan*, "Greece" (c).

84

In modern practice, the *yod* makes up the other half of the full spelling arsenal. Like the *vav*, it is a vowel *indicator*, but not a carrier, too, like the *aleph* or *ayin*. It cannot initiate the *i* vowel at the start of a word or syllable, but it can indicate its presence in most cases. The relevant vowel sign – almost always implicit in its pointing – is a dot below the carrying consonant, known as a *Hiriq*. Followed by the *yod*, the combination is a *Hiriq malé*; without it, it is a *Hiriq Haser*.

The *yod* can also be found in most instances of vowel compounds denoting the long *i* sound, as in *pie*. In an echo of the diaeresis (umlaut) in words such as *naïve* or the double *i* in common misspellings of Latin plurals such as *cactii*, this is often indicated by a double *yod*. A typical occurrence of this in native words is the suffix *iim*, which is the standard indication of a pair or a double (e.g., *einiim* = eyes, *ozniim* = ears, etc.). In transliterated foreign words or names, the double yod can also indicate the long *a* sound (as in *day*). But don't count on all *ay* or *aï* sounds being signposted in this way: many common Hebrew words with those sounds sport only one *yod* (Fig. 58).

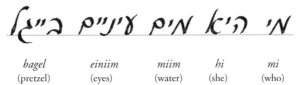

| bagel | einiim | miim | hi | mi |
| (pretzel) | (eyes) | (water) | (she) | (who) |

Fig. 58  The many uses of *yod* as a vowel indicator. In Hebrew words the double *yod* is usually pronounced "eye"; in foreign words and names, it can also represent a long *a* as in *bagel*.

Finally, don't forget that, like all Hebrew characters, *yod* is first and foremost a consonant and is therefore used wherever *y* is required.

85

## *l*

The cursive Hebrew *lamed* is conceptually different from the Roman *l* but curiously ends up being fairly similar. It is drawn with a small loop at the foot of the letter and goes from the bottom up rather than from the top down as its Mirror Roman counterpart would suggest. The top of the letter is then free to "flap in the wind," provided it does not cross back over the ascender, as this would confuse it with one or two other letters, as we shall see later.

*haleluiah*

Fig. 59 The cursive Hebrew *lamed* is drawn from the bottom up (b) rather than top down, as the Mirror Roman *l* would suggest (a). Unlike the Greek ∂, which it superficially resembles, the letter has a little loop at the bottom that is only nominally observed (c).

## *s (1)*

The *s* is an interesting case, as somewhere between Greece and Rome its lower half got twisted around. The original Canaanite form (Fig. 60-a) looked like *w*, which the Greeks characteristically turned 90° to create the familiar Greek sigma (Σ). Even in its Square Hebrew guise (Fig. 60-b) we can see something of the original concept.

The cursive *shin* (pron. *sheen*, but quickly) is easily understood if you imagine writing a capital *E* lying on its back – which the Square form resembles – in one flowing, clockwise movement (Fig. 60).

c                b     a

Fig. 60   The Modern Hebrew Cursive *shin* (c) is essentially the result of writing the Square form (b) quickly, the pen sweeping back after the basic bowl to create the middle member. Unlike a normal lowercase *e*, however, it goes clockwise and projects above most other letters.

As you might guess from its name, however, the *shin's* default value is *sh* rather than *s* (statistically, by a factor of ten to one).[7] When pointing is explicit, the distinction is made by a dot: to its upper right if it is *sh*, to its upper left if it is *s* (hence the latter's name: *shin smalit* = left-handed *shin*). When pointing is omitted, however, the assumption is it is *sh*, unless you know otherwise. Where it can be read either way, the context tells you which, and only if that fails is a dot placed as appropriate, e.g., to distinguish ***sharah*** (she sings) from *Sarah* (Sarah) or indeed *sarah* (woman cabinet minister).

When an unambiguous *s* is called for (for example, when transliterating foreign words or names), a different letter is used – the *sammeç* – which is next.

### *S* (2)

The role of the plain-vanilla *s* in Hebrew is played by the *sammeç* (pron. ***sam-mekh***), which we mentioned in passing earlier. It is drawn just like the Roman *o* – a counterclockwise circle (or, if you prefer, much like the lowercase Greek letter *sigma*: σ – Fig. 61).

87

| *sucot* | *sport* | *sinai / sini* | *student* |
| (Succoth) | (sports) | (Sinai / Chinese) | (student) |

Fig. 61    The letter *sammeç* is written just like the normal Roman *o*.

How this came about is a bit of a mystery. Its original Phoenician/ Old Hebrew form couldn't have been more different: a *t*-like character with two or three cross-strokes (Fig. 4) – a form which in due course inspired the Roman *X*. So there's nothing for it but to learn it the old-fashioned way (the third such letter so far).

Once you get used to it, though, its implementation is very easy: the *sammeç* represents the plain *s* in virtually all transliterated foreign words or names (e.g., *sport, student*, etc. – Fig. 61), as well as in many native words.

## *t* (1)

You may have noticed in your Mirror Roman practice that the *t* has a strong tendency to develop a "foot" leading on to the next letter (Fig. 62-b). This is natural and has echoes in the lowercase *t* of many Roman typefaces. We also see it in its cousin, the lowercase Greek *tau* (τ) to this day.

In the Hebrew *tav* this foot is not only acceptable but essential, in order to distinguish it from the *Het* – so indulge it. You'll note the cross-stroke also seems inclined to be more than just a short horizontal stroke, so carry that through, too, to form a complete *resh*-stroke (Fig. 62-c).

88

d          c             b        a

Fig. 62 The cursive *tav* (c) is a natural resolution of the Mirror Roman *t* (b). The overlaps are normally trimmed, and the order of strokes switched to suit the direction of writing (d).

*Et voilà.* You've pretty well made a typical Hebrew *tav,* except that, for the sake of tidiness, you should also trim back the overlaps of the two strokes (Fig. 62-d). Also, since we are writing right to left, make the *resh-*stroke first.

The thing to bear in mind is that *tav* is one of two *t* letters in Hebrew (the other is *Tet,* which we shall come to in a moment). In the Bible, you can easily tell which is which in the original Hebrew: the *tav* is the one transliterated as *th*: e.g., *Bethlehem, Bathsheba, Jonathan, Esther,* etc. Modern research suggests that in those days the letter's soft version (as per the *beged cefet* rule) may well have been pronounced like the English *th* (as in *thing*). In the modern vernacular, however, that distinction has been lost, and it is pronounced as a plain *t* in all circumstances. In fact, these days when a *th* sound is expressly needed (as in transliterated foreign names or words) an apostrophe-like accent is added above to indicate it.

Following this biblical tradition, the modern practice generally reciprocates and uses *tav* to represent all instances of *th* in foreign words and names (Fig. 63).

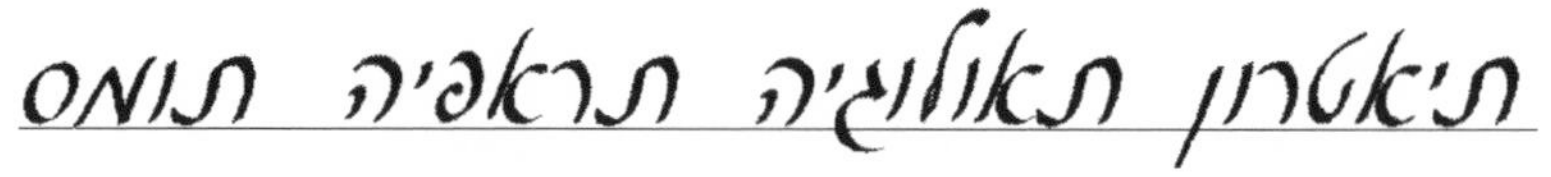

תיאטרון תאולוגיה תרפיה תומס

| | | | |
|---|---|---|---|
| *tomas* | *terapia* | *teologiah* | *teatron* |
| (Thomas) | (therapy) | (theology) | (theater) |

Fig. 63 The *tav* is usually used to represent *th* in Hebraized versions or transliterations of foreign words and names.

*t* *(2)*

The second Hebrew *t* – the *Tet* – was originally invented by the ancient Canaanites to represent the guttural variation of that sound. In modern Israel, the guttural pronunciation has disappeared in all but Yemen-born Jews, but in ancient times it was almost certainly de rigueur. However, since ancient Egyptian (not a Semitic language) did not have such a character, *Tet* started life as an improvised *tav* with a circle around it (Fig. 64-a). Being surplus to European requirements, however, it was dropped by the Romans entirely, which is why there is no counterpart for you to work from.

However, it is fairly simple. Over the centuries, scribes grew tired of drawing a circle with bits in it and so opened it up to create a one-stroke, diameter-line-with-open-circle sort of sign (Fig. 64-b), which eventually was simplified further to create the Square Hebrew form (Fig. 64-c).

d    c    b    a

Fig. 64     The evolution of the *Tet*

In the modern cursive the open end has broken free from orbit and created a tall letter (Fig. 64-d and Fig. 65) – similar to the *shin* only without the loop back at the top. The result is also a little like a normal Roman *t* without the cross-stroke, something Israeli graphic artists often exploit when transliterating words such as *diet* in the Hebrew graphics for drink labels. Strictly speaking, though, it is more curved, and – more importantly – it is drawn from four o'clock, not noon, the better to go with the flow of right-to-left writing.

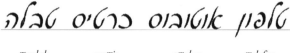

| *Tavlah* | *carTis* | *oTobus* | *Telefon* |
|---|---|---|---|
| (table in doc.) | (card) | (bus) | (telephone) |

Fig. 65  The *Tet* is the letter of choice when transliterating plain *t* (vs. *th*) of foreign terms.

To you, as a Roman-script native, the particular significance of *Tet* is that, in addition to featuring in many Hebrew words, it is the character of choice when representing the plain *t* in foreign words and names – e.g., *Telefon*, *oTobus* (bus), *carTis* (card), *Tavlah* (table, as in documents), *demoqraTiah*, *proTesTanTi*, etc. (Fig. 65).

**z**

*"Horizontal strokes are tolerated only in the direction of the writing hand." (*Sixth Rule of Chirodynamics*)*

The cursive Hebrew *zayin* is perhaps the clearest example of a Hebrew cursive emerging from the resolution of its Mirror Roman counterpart. The top and bottom strokes of the Mirror Roman *z* are awkward (Fig. 66-a) as they move away from the writing hand, so the real cursive *zayin* fixes this by turning the top horizontal into a tilted stroke and by merging the bottom one with its main diagonal into a single curved sweep (Fig. 66-b) – much like the *gimmel* in reverse, and with the same tendency to dip below the baseline.

b                    a

Fig. 66    The cursive Hebrew *zayin* is essentially a resolved Mirror Roman *z*.

## Happy Accidents (*c*, *e*, *f*)

## *c (k)*

In Part I we mentioned in passing how the character that appears to have survived the direction switch virtually unchanged, and is therefore the easiest to learn, is in fact nothing but a serendipitous fluke.

As we see in Fig. 12 (p. 31) and in Fig. 67-a (below), the original Old Hebrew/Phoenician *caf* looked a lot like its true descendant – the Roman lowercase *k* – only upside-down. During its Aramaic phase and thereafter, this character somehow became increasingly fudged – most likely because its diagonal nature clashed with the neat square template that was being imposed. Over time, essential characteristics were confused with ornament and vice versa, to the point where it eventually morphed beyond recognition into what happens to be a square-ish mirror image of the Roman *c* (Fig. 67-b).

c          b          a

Fig. 67   The image of the original Old Hebrew and Phoenician *caf* (a) still lives on (albeit upside down) in its true Roman descendant – *k* – whereas the Square Hebrew version (b) somehow evolved into a near-mirror image of the Roman *c*.

No matter – for our purposes the similarity is too good to throw away. Doubly so, since the two letters also share a tendency to lose their hard *k* sound in certain grammatical situations. The difference is that while in European languages the soft *c* (such as before *e* or *i*) is pronounced like *s* or *ts* or *ch*, the soft *caf* (*caf rafah* in Hebrew) is pronounced like the German *ch* and applies everywhere except at the start of words or after a closed syllable (like other *beged cefet* consonants). As a result, in speech it is sometimes confused with the *Het*, although in theory it sounds a little harsher.

Although *caf*'s graphic resemblance to *c* makes the initial transition easier, the Hebrew Academy has decreed that it should not be used when transliterating a hard *c* in foreign words and names because of its tendency to "go soft" under some conditions.  Instead, the *quf* (Fig. 55) should be used. Notable exceptions to this rule are words starting with a hard *ch* (e.g., *chrome, chronology*): these are usually of Greek origin, and the relevant Greek letter (*chi* – χ) has a similar guttural sound and was used to represent the Hebrew *caf* when the Old Testament was translated into Greek in the second century CE. Thus, the Hebrew for *chirodynam-*

93

*ics – çirodinamiqah* – would use *caf* to represent the first *c*, but *quf* for the second one (Fig. 68).

| | | |
|---|---|---|
| *çronologiah* | *çroni* | *çimiah* |
| (chronology) | (chronic) | (chemistry) |

Fig. 68 The *ch* in words of Greek origin are, by tradition, transliterated using the letter *caf*. The rules of Hebrew grammar decree that a *caf* at the start of words must always be hard, but in practice most Hebrew speakers use its soft (guttural) form.

As with *péh* and *bet*, only a dot in its center distinguishes the hard *caf* from its soft variety, which is omitted except in full dots-and-dashes regalia and in situations where there is risk of ambiguity (Fig. 69-a). However, at the end of words, a special terminal form – the *caf sophit* (Fig. 69-b-c) – is used, which is *always* soft (Fig. 69).

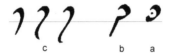

Fig. 69 A dot is placed in the center of a hard *caf* in explicit pointing and wherever there is risk of reading it as soft (a). Its terminal form (*caf sophit* – b) is always used at the end of words: this is essentially the same character, plus a downstroke that goes below the baseline (b), although in practice more fluid forms occur (c).

*e*

Actually, this is a bit of a cheat, but it settles an old score. As a graphic entity, the letter *E* is a European vowel forged from a fully paid-up Semitic consonant. Originally, it represented the plain aspirated *h*, or *héh*, of Phoenician/Old Hebrew (Fig. 70-a). It is only fitting, therefore, that today it provides the opportunity to do something equally blatant and introduce a letter that has no European counterpart. This is the letter *ayin*, which we mentioned earlier in connection with the letter *o*.

Fig. 70   The lowercase Mirror Roman *E* (b) is a little awkward, but upside down it presents no chirodynamic difficulties (d) and happens to represents the Hebrew character *ayin*.

In purely graphic terms, the modern cursive *ayin* can be thought of as an upside-down Script-style *e* (Fig. 70-d). In fact, the passing resemblance of its printed form to the capital *E* (Fig. 94) was probably a factor in the decision by Jews in medieval central Europe to use *ayin* to represent the *e* vowel in the Yiddish script (which in all other respects is identical to the Hebrew one).

In Hebrew proper, however, the *ayin* is a vowel carrier like the *aleph*, and as such is not committed to any particular vowel sound.

Given that it has a similar role to the *aleph*, what is the *ayin* for? The answer is that it is supposed to have a guttural sound, as in Arabic. Like other such letters, however, in the speech of most Hebrew speakers today that distinction is ignored. As a result, certain words that may sound the same in common speech and in Roman transliteration (*al, im, et, ani, ma'arav*, etc.) are in fact quite distinct both in spelling and in meaning.

95

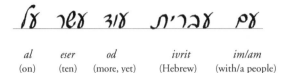

| al | eser | od | ivrit | im/am |
|----|------|-----|-------|-------|
| (on) | (ten) | (more, yet) | (Hebrew) | (with/a people) |

Fig. 71  Like the *aleph*, *ayin* is a vowel carrier, but strictly speaking with a guttural kick.

As a purely Semitic character, the *ayin* is almost never called upon when transliterating foreign words or names (unless they're Arabic), nor is it associated with any particular vowel by default, as the neutral *aleph* is with short *a*. As a result, the short *e* vowel has no letter that may act as its indicator in Hebrew. The only way to signal its presence, when not evident from the context or conjugation, is by its explicit pointing symbol: three dots in an upside-down pyramid arrangement known as a *ségol*.

Fig. 72  In the absence of a Hebrew letter to indicate the short *e* sound, its explicit vowel symbol – *ségol* – must be used in situations where the reading is ambiguous, e.g., the word *Hevel* (rope), which without the *ségol*s or contextual clues might be read as *Haval* (that's a pity).

# *f*

*F* in Hebrew does not exist as an independent letter, but only as the soft version of the letter *péh* (Fig. 38). This occurs only at specific grammatical junctures and graphically looks no different, except at the end of words, when it is called *péh sophit* (terminal *péh*) and is *always f*-sounding.

The Greeks, as we said, created their own *f* letter (ɸ) to use wherever they pleased. The Romans agreed with the sentiment but rejected the graphic form of the ɸ character in favor of one which their immediate predecessors, the Etruscans, fashioned out of the Phoenician/Old Hebrew *vav* (whose position in the alphabet it also usurped, dispatching the actual *v* to the end).

In another instance of supreme serendipity, this form happens to bear a strong likeness to the Square Hebrew *péh sophit* – to an extent that carries through to the cursive forms of both scripts (Fig. 73).

Fig. 73  The horizontal right-to-left cross-stroke is the only real problem with the Mirror Roman *f* (a); the solution is to draw the figure in one swoop from the bottom, looping back and across from the top (b). This corresponds to the *f*-sounding cursive *péh sophit*.

Drawn from the top down as in normal Roman, the Mirror Roman *f* presents no particular chirodynamic difficulties (Fig. 73-a), except for the cross-stroke, which naturally tends to go from left to right but would thereby lead us in the wrong direction.

Fig. 74  Variations on the *péh sophit* theme include mirrored ß-like figures (b) and anything else where the final loop points downwards.

97

The solution is to draw the character in one swoop from the bottom up – like a *lamed* – and loop it back at the top to create a right-to-left cross-stroke. The latter feels all right, provided it is drawn on the diagonal rather than horizontally (Fig. 73-b). Finish off with a slight swirl down and back to the upstroke, and the result is the classic cursive *péh sophit* (Fig. 74-a).

In all other positions in a word, *f* is represented by a standard *péh* (Fig. 74-c, Fig. 75):

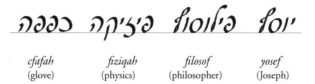

| *cfafah* | *fiziqah* | *filosof* | *yosef* |
|----------|-----------|-----------|---------|
| (glove) | (physics) | (philosopher) | (Joseph) |

Fig. 75  Only at the end of words does the *f*-sounding soft *péh* acquire a distinct form (*yosef, filosof*). Elsewhere a standard *péh* is used, and the *f* sound is either inferred from the rules of Hebrew grammar (e.g., *cfafah*) or – in the case of words of foreign origin – simply known (*fiziqah, februar*).

## Wallflowers (*j, w, x, tz*)

### *j*

Like *w* and *x*, the *j* is an invention that came long after the adoption of the Canaanite alphabet by the ancient Greeks. Indeed, it only became a letter in its own right in the sixteenth century CE.

Consequently it has no Hebrew equivalent, at least not as it is pronounced in English. Native Hebrew words don't use the *j* sound at all, and foreign words of that sort that have been formally adopted into the language use a *y* sound instead (e.g., *proyect*). The biblical names that one associates with the letter (e.g., *Jacob, Joshua, Jerusalem, Elijah, Jesus*) are likewise derivations of *yod* in the original Hebrew. Thus Jacob = *Yaacov*, Joshua = *Yehoshua*, Jerusalem = *Yerushaliim*, Elijah = *Eliyahu*, and Jesus = *Yeshu*.

b          a

Fig. 76  Chirodynamically, Mirror Roman *j* (a) feels okay, but looks too much like *ayin*. However, this is not an issue as it has no ready Hebrew equivalent anyway, and a *gimmel* with an apostrophe-like accent is used instead (b).

This is just as well, since the Mirror Roman *j* (Fig. 76-a) looks too much like the Hebrew *ayin*, which is already spoken for. So the letter *gimmel* is used instead, with an apostrophe-like accent placed above (Fig. 76-b and Fig. 77).

John/Jon      jerrycan      jazz

Fig. 77  Examples of *j* words or names commonly encountered in modern Hebrew vernacular

## *w*

When they handed out the consonants to the Semitic languages, there was only one *v* and one *w* in stock: Hebrew got the *v* and Arabic got the *w*. However, unlike other nonnative sounds such as the English

99

*th*, the *w* sound is readily recognized and pronounceable by native Hebrew speakers. As its English or French name suggests, it is represented literally as a double-*u* or -*v*, namely, two consecutive *vavs* (Fig. 78).

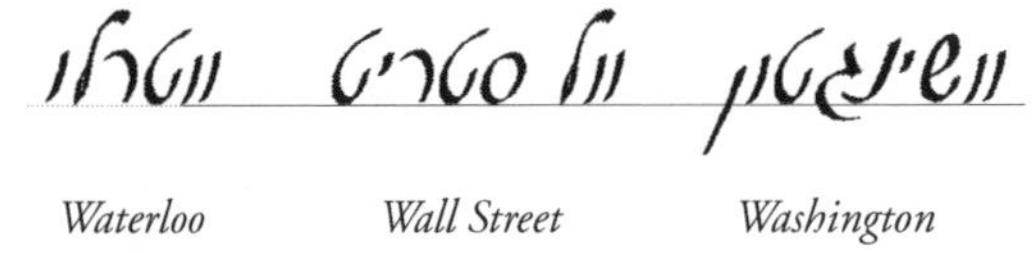

*Waterloo*          *Wall Street*          *Washington*

Fig. 78  When followed by an *o* or *u* sound, the second *vav* in the double-*vav* representation doubles up as the vowel indicator. Three consecutive vavs are not allowed.

To minimize problems caused by the absence of a proper letter for the *w* sound in foreign words that have irrevocably entered the modern Hebrew lexicon, *w* is treated as a *v*, as in German – thus, *vatt* (watt), *vals* (waltz), *vaffel* (waffle), *sendvich* (sandwich) etc. Nevertheless, as you can imagine, what with the *vav*'s other hats, difficulties can and do arise in transliterating foreign words or names where *w* is followed by an *o* or *u* sound. If your name is "Woe," for example, you face the prospect of your name in Hebrew being reduced to three small vertical lines.[*] Only you can't, because – just to make matters more interesting – only two consecutive *vav*s are ever tolerated (the line had to be drawn somewhere). In these situations, one must rely on prior knowledge of the correct pronunciation – or even (gasp!) employ the Roman-script original (Fig. 78).

## *x*

*X* has no single-character Hebrew equivalent. Instead, the *ks* sound is

---

[*]    Of course, if Woe is you, that's probably the least of your problems.

100

achieved by the pair *quf-sammeç*, or (in words or names of Greek origin) *caf-sammeç* (Fig. 79).

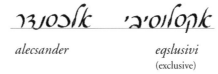

*alecsander*          *eqslusivi*
                      (exclusive)

Fig. 79  *X* is generally represented by the pair *quf-sammeç*. The use of *caf-sammeç* (e.g., *alecsander*) is reserved for words or names of Greek origin.

### *tz*

Just as the Roman alphabet has a single character for *ks*, Hebrew has always had a dedicated sign for the *ts* or *tz* sound, which both the Greeks and the Romans decided to do without. This is the *tzadi*.

Shaped like a large *3*, the cursive *tzadi* may strike you at first as much like the cursive *dalet* (Fig. 80-a), and you would be right, but it is markedly bigger – projecting above most letters – and completes a full curve on the baseline, rather than landing smack into it (Fig. 80-b). It is also the fifth and last of the letters to have a distinct form at the end of words (Fig. 80-c).

*tzaf*      *tzatz*      c      b      a
(floats)    (pops up)

Fig. 80  The *tzadi* differs visibly from the cursive *dalet* (a), both in size and in completion (b). Its terminal version (c) resembles the terminal *péh* except its final flourish must loop up rather than down – as illustrated by the words *tzatz* vs. *tzaf*.

101

Other examples:

$$חול3ה \ 3יון \ י3חק \ 3דוקי$$

| | | | |
|---|---|---|---|
| *tzdoqi* | *yitzHaq* | *tzion* | *Hutzpah* |
| (Sadducee) | (Isaac) | (Zion) | (insolence) |

Fig. 81    Examples of Hebrew words and names featuring *tzadi*

With an added apostrophe, the *tzadi* also represents the English *ch* (*tch*) sound in borrowed words such as *check*, *chips*, etc. – since Hebrew has no native equivalent. (The pairing *Tet-shin* could be used, in theory, but the result might be read as a proper Hebrew word with an implicit vowel in between, so it is generally avoided – Fig. 82).

$$3'פס \ 3ק \ 3רלס$$

| | | |
|---|---|---|
| *chips* | *cheq* | *charls* |
| (chips/fries) | (bank check) | (Charles) |

Fig. 82  Examples of *tzadi*-with-apostrophe representing the *ch* (*tch*) sound in foreign terms

## Summary

That's about the size of it. Having reviewed both alphabets, you should now have the essential tools with which to write in Hebrew characters. As you can see, the biggest challenge is not so much mastering the letters themselves as understanding and implementing Hebrew's treatment of vowels.

From here on it is a matter of practice, and of spelling. Spelling native Hebrew words involves a knowledge of the language itself and in particular the roots of words – the three-consonant "skeletons," or frames, underlying every native Hebrew word that tell you when to use *aleph* or *ayin*, *Tet* or *tav*, *quf* or *caf*, etc. An in-depth discussion of Hebrew word roots is outside the scope of this book, but you can see instances of these in our passage from the book of Genesis, as set out in Modern Hebrew Cursive (Fig. 83).

With no Hebrew roots to adhere to, far greater leniency is extended to the spelling of foreign words and names, but the general rule, as we said, is that you use *Tet* to represent plain *t*; *tav* for *th*; *quf* for all instances of hard *c*, *k*, and *q*; and *caf* for all hard and guttural instances of *ch* (e.g., *choreography*, *Bach*). Remember that vowels must always be supported (i.e., preceded) by a consonant: in the absence of one, in foreign words or names an *aleph* is always used (followed by a vowel indicator such as *yod* for *i* sounds or *vav* for *o* or *u*). In addition to the words already used for illustration hitherto, you can try your hand at the examples provided in the appendix.

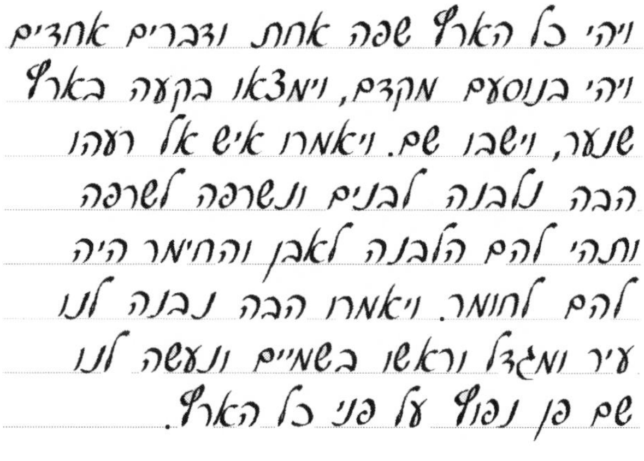

Fig. 83  First verses of the book of Genesis 11 in Modern Hebrew Cursive

103

# Part III

*From Writing to Reading*

# From Cursive to Square

The transition from *writing* Hebrew to reading it is first and foremost about moving from the cursive to the classic Square Hebrew forms. This is implied in the latter's common name (*otiot dfus* = print letters), and the key to learning them is to understand that they are *what the cursive forms are trying to express in one or two strokes*, in the quest for more fluid and quicker writing. This is rather like playing *Jeopardy*, or guessing a question from its answer: there are a number of equally plausible possibilities, you can have fun trying, and whichever one proves to be correct is sure to make sense.

However, you needn't guess what the Square characters look like, as I will tell you. Here, there is no need for conjecture, unorthodox reconstructions, or imaginary bridges across linguistic divides. How and why the change occurred in each case is fairly well known.

## The distractions of typography

Typography can get in the way of discerning essential forms. In any given script, the design of lettering is determined by the medium used to create its historic prototype. In China and Japan it was the paintbrush. In Rome it was the chisel, since the examples held up by the early master printers in Europe as the quintessential forms of the Roman script were the Latin inscriptions on stone monuments scattered around the Roman empire – in particular, those at the base of Trajan's Column in Rome. In

Hebrew it was the reed pen or quill, on parchment or paper – in a tradition established during the early Second Temple period (third century BCE) and carried on through centuries of careful replicating of innumerous biblical and Talmudic texts by professional scribes.

a                                                                      b

Fig. 84  The contrasting typographies of traditional Roman and Hebrew scripts are
due to the different media used in the historic prototype. In the case of
Roman script this was Latin stone inscriptions (a), whereas in Hebrew it
stemmed from writing Scripture in ink with a cut reed, or quill, on parchment or paper (b).

The result was widely differing aesthetics. While Western typography still subscribes to the notions of beauty and authority established by the Roman stonemasons – verticals thicker than horizontals, stroke ends finished off with thin "feet" (known as serifs) – the design of Square Hebrew letters was influenced by the angle of the hand, direction of writing, and cut of the nib of Scriptural scribes.[8] By the late Middle Ages this had resulted in thin verticals and solid horizontal blocks, or "handles," at the top and bottom of letters – with an optional, vertically inclined curly flourish where the pen first hits paper.

Such purely stylistic features add to the unfamiliarity of a foreign script to newcomers and can make the task of learning it more difficult.

However, when you strip these away and bare the essential forms of the characters, it is easier to appreciate their true forms and to assimilate them in your mind.

Fortunately, modern Hebrew typography comes to our aid, as it has modified the traditional style and in some cases even reversed its traditional esthetic, in a bid for graphic compatibility with established Roman script typefaces. Character handles have been eliminated or made more subtle, and the thickness of vertical and horizontal strokes made nearly or actually equivalent – in effect re-establishing the practice prior to the tenth century CE. As a result, Israelis today associate the traditional style almost exclusively with prayer books, Bibles, and the Diaspora and are therefore amused when they see it used in Hebrew signs at foreign airports or on labels, etc., to provide mundane information such as nutritional details or directions to the nearest diaper-changing station.

### Working back from the cursive

Square Hebrew may have been fine for Scripture – in fact, it was compulsory – but for everyday use it was as laborious as writing EXCLUSIVELY IN ROMAN CAPITALS was for the Christian monks and scribes of the Middle Ages. The emergence of the various handwriting styles and cursives in both scripts during this period thus reflects a shared urge to depict the classical forms in one or two fluid pen strokes.

As we shall see, in over half the twenty-seven signs of the Hebrew alphabet (including the five special terminal forms), this "reverse engineering" is quite straightforward, if not trivial. In most of the others it makes sense once you try it for yourself. Only in three – the *aleph*, *lamed*, and *mem* – does the difference defy any immediately obvious graphic explanation and require some historical background. Not too bad a record, when you consider similar discrepancies in the Roman script between the upper- and lowercase forms of *A*, *B*, *D*, *G*, *H*, *N*, *Q*, and *R* – not to mention the differences between roman (print) and italic versions of **a** and *a*, **g** and *g*, etc.

As we are no longer discussing the letters with reference to their Roman equivalents, we shall now review them in their proper Hebrew alphabetical order (which is good for you to know in any case). In each instance, the cursive form that we have learned is shown to the left of two typical modern Square Hebrew typefaces (Fig. 85 and Fig. 86).

*Pninim* (Fig. 85) is a modern variation of the traditional typefaces usually associated with Square Hebrew since the dawn of Hebrew printing. Horizontals are thicker than the verticals, and the handles are chunky and slightly stylized, though less so than the traditional prayer book style. This or similar typefaces is still the standard in newspapers and most books.

אבגדהוזחטיכדלמםנסעפפצץקשת

Fig. 85  The Pninim font is a modern variation of the traditional Square Hebrew print typeface.

*Ariel* (Fig. 86) is characteristic of the sans-serif (serif-less) Hebrew typefaces invented only in modern times. Fonts like Ariel (a play on Arial, the common Roman script font) feature in short or informative texts such as signs and captions and in some word processing and websites. In keeping with their sans-serif Roman counterparts (with which they are often juxtaposed), horizontal and vertical strokes are nearly uniform in thickness, handles and serifs are subtle or nonexistent, and formal distinctions between similar-looking characters are maximized for greater legibility.

אבגדהוזחטיכרלממנסעפפצצקשת

Fig. 86 The *Ariel* typeface is typical of sans-serif Hebrew fonts invented in the modern era.

---

## aleph         *k* **א** **א**

As we said in the introduction to this chapter, *aleph* is one of three characters whose Square form seems to have little to do with its cursive. However, although it isn't immediately obvious, there is a logic to the evolution that took place.

The source of the problem was the fact that the Square version uses three very discrete strokes. Distilling these into two wasn't easy, but over time it was achieved, after a fashion, by extending the leftmost stroke to the top of, and eventually beyond, the main diagonal and merging the right one with the latter to create a *k*-like character (Fig. 87).[9]

Fig. 87 The cursive *aleph* (far left) evolved from the desire to reduce the three strokes of the Square form (far right) to two.

Ironically, as you now know, the end result looks a lot like the Old Hebrew form, which makes one wonder why the Aramaic ventured so far from the original in the first place. But that's paleography for you.

## *bet* בבּ

Some letters are best understood in terms of what they are trying hard *not* to be. The *bet* is such a letter. Throughout its history as a Square Hebrew character, its main concern has always been how not to be confused with the *caf,* which is similar only without the little tail in the back (Fig. 88-a).

The same problem dogged the cursive form, of course. In the textbook modern cursive, as we've seen (above, third from right), the letter's "non-*caf*ness" is signified by a small arch in the bottom stroke. Originally, however, the idea was to accommodate the tail in one flowing stroke with the rest of the letter. This eventually became a kink along the back (Fig. 88-b), creating an almost capital *B*-like character without the stem.

d    c    b    a

Fig. 88  Different methods of expressing the tail led to variations in the cursive *bet* over the centuries.

In the German Hebrew cursive that followed centuries later, this was abridged still further to a *2*-like character (Fig. 88-c), which can still be seen in some people's handwriting, but the "rebound arch" form (Fig. 88-

d) is now the official prototype.

## gimmel                               ڌ ג ג

When cursive *gimmel* is placed next to its Square versions, the relationship between the cursive form and its parent is obvious. Once the Square form was drawn in one go, it was natural for the "front leg" to be carried on into a curved flourish. The result was so distinctive that the flourish has since become the dominant feature (Fig. 89).

Fig. 89  The cursive *gimmel* evolved naturally from drawing the Square form in one stroke – then indulging the end flourish.

## dalet                               ʒ ד ד

The square template of Aramaic/Square Hebrew means the distinctions between different letters are occasionally subtle. The print form of *dalet* is one such example: its similarity to the printed *resh* is such that it relies entirely on a small rear projection to avoid confusion.

Freed from the square template straightjacket, the cursive form indulged this feature. Over time, this quick double-back (Fig. 90-a) evolved into a gaplike feature that was ultimately made official and fixed into a short loop.

c        b         a

Fig. 90 The cursive *dalet* came about from incorporating the top-rear projection into a single pen stroke, eventually making a feature of the gap that tended to form.

## *héh*        ה ה הּ

A classic illustration of how Square Hebrew got its name, the Square *héh* is exactly as one would expect from its cursive. If they were all like this, we'd be laughing.

## *vav*        ו ו ו

The word *vav* means "hook," and true to this denotation since Canaanite times, most Square versions of this letter recognize that the handle at the top is not merely a calligraphic ornament and have therefore retained it. In other respects, however, it is much the same *i*-like character we know from the cursive.

## *zayin*        ז ז ז

The short projection of the top cross-bar to the right means that the standard Square *zayin* (far right) must keep its left projection short, too — to avoid confusion with the *dalet*. At the same time, the projection to the

114

right is essential, to avoid confusion with the Square *vav*. Small wonder, then, that even modern typefaces like the Ariel (above, second from right) introduce subtle bends into the stem to reinforce the *zayin*'s distinct identity.

These bends or kinks also featured in handwritten styles down the ages, for the same reason. The modern cursive *zayin* is the result of indulging these into a full curving sweep, at which point the little "hat" became unnecessary. Coincidentally, this also brought it closer to the Roman *z* and to its ancestral form (Fig. 91).

**Fig. 91** The kink in the *zayin*'s stem is useful in promoting its distinctiveness. In handwritten cursive this eventually became the main feature, and the little "hat" was dropped.

### Het

Self-explanatory.

### Tet

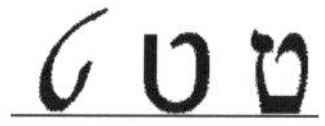

As discussed in Part II, hints of *Tet*'s origins as a circle-with-a-diagonal can still be seen in its printed form. Although the cursive form focuses more on the tall upstroke at the end, all printed varieties preserve a remnant of the old diagonal, in what is otherwise a simple *u*-like shape.

115

## *yod* ＇＂ ＇  ＇

Although we have likened it to an elongated dot of the lowercase *i*, purists rightly criticize the drop of the small horizontal handle at the top of the Square *yod* in sans-serif typefaces like Ariel (above, second from right). As in the *vav*, this handle has always been an integral part of its Square form, and the creators of most modern Square typefaces have taken care to make it more than a jumped-up apostrophe, as might be said of the cursive form. Indeed, in some traditionally-inspired fonts it is the top handle blob that predominates, relegating the vertical bit to the status of an insignificant appendage.

## *caf* כ כ כ

## *caf sophit* ך ך ך

The ordinary printed *caf* is much as we would imagine, given its cursive offspring. Its printed terminal form, however, differs from the cursive in that it drops straight down from the top bar instead of completing or nearly completing the *c*-like shape. Length is critical here: it must always extend beyond the baseline, to avoid being read as a *resh*.

## *lamed*

The *lamed* represents perhaps the most dramatic departure of a cursive letter from its original Square form.

Fig. 92 The "flagpole" of the *lamed* – the dominant feature of the original Canaanite letter (a) – gradually diminished during its Aramaic phase in favor of the part below the horizontal bar (b). In informal writing, however, it reasserted itself (d).

The clue is in its little "flag-pole" at the top. *Lamed* is the only Hebrew letter to project above the "roof line" of all other members of the Square Hebrew alphabet (a perennial headache in the design of electronic displays). Initially this projection was in fact its dominant feature, with the bit below the horizontal bar either nonexistent or a mere afterthought – in effect an *L*-like character with a tail (Fig. 92-a). In fact, it *was* an *L*: like all Canaanite letters it, too, was mirrored when the Greeks switched the direction of writing, but reverted to its original form when this was found to be easier in left-to-right writing. Over the centuries this tail inexplicably grew in size and importance to the point where the letter became more like a *7* with a mere "forelock" (Fig. 92-b).

Released from the confines of the Square template, the cursive *lamed*'s projection quickly recaptured its original importance. Like an uncoiled spring, it merged with the horizontal segment to create an elon-

117

gated *S*-like character, with the bit underneath the bar symbolically bundled into a small loop at the base, undoing much of its evolution under its Aramaic/Square Hebrew guise. At some point, people began to draw the letter from the bottom up, as this leaves one in a better position for the next letter when writing from right to left (Fig. 92-d).

## *mem*                                   מ ם א

## *mem sophit*                            ם ם ק

After a promising start in its ordinary cursive form, the Square *mem* seems bent on making mischief. Not content with having a terminal version that is quite different from its standard form in the cursive, the printed versions of both the standard and terminal forms also seem to have little in common with each other or with their cursive counterparts.

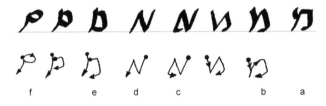

Fig. 93                    The many faces of *mem*

A closer look at the standard Square *mem* (Fig. 93-a) reveals why its cursive version had such problems. With its triangular/trapezoid body and "teapot spout," it is probably the trickiest letter of the Hebrew alpha-

118

bet to express in one or two strokes. The most obvious approach – combine the spout with the rest of the body (Fig. 93-b) – was a popular compromise for a while, but since this went against the grain of right-to-left writing, a mirrored variation of this emerged instead (Fig. 93-c). With a further simplification – abandoning the tiny backstroke in the triangle – the modern form was born (Fig. 93-d).

The printed terminal *mem* might be said to be the ultimate Square Hebrew letter, in that it is essentially a plain square. This represents the logical conclusion of a parallel scenario that beckoned the character around the first century BCE, when it hovered between a closed and open version (Fig. 93-e). Over time, however, it lost the little spout of the ordinary *mem* (although there is still a hint of it in the traditional typeface), as it never could decide whether this was an essential feature or merely an ornament. Meanwhile, the *p*-like form of its cursive version is the result of yet another interpretation (Fig. 93-f) of the same idea.

Such is the story of *mem*, The Letter That Couldn't Decide What It Looked Like.

---

*nun*

*nun sophit*

The desire to create a virtual horizontal bar at the top and bottom of lines of text, so beloved of Hebrew scribes in the past millennium, meant that handles were often added to the tops of letters even when not part of

119

their essential makeup. The *nun* is a classic example – however, the top handle of its Square form is kept short, lest it be confused with *caf*. Traditional typefaces minimize this risk by adding a kink to the stem (above, right), but sans-serif fonts such as Ariel (above, middle) iron it out again while – oddly – keeping the top handle.

The cursive version, as we have seen, sensibly drops the top handle altogether and focuses on the letter's bend at the bottom, which *is* an essential characteristic.

All of which applies to the printed terminal *nun*, too. Like most other terminal forms, it must extend below the baseline, not least to avoid confusion with the *vav*. Here, too, the kink in the traditional typeface is an advantage not retained in most sans-serif ones.

## *sammeç*                               *O O ࠐ*

The *o*-like letter of the cursive is revealed in its traditional form (far right) to be in fact an asymmetrical character, with a straight horizontal bar topping a *u*-like lower section that pulls slightly to the left.

## *ayin*                               *ɤ ט ט*

Like many other letters, the cursive form of the *ayin* makes eminent sense once you attempt the Square form in one quick, uninterrupted pen stroke. In fact, it is a perfect illustration of the Third Rule of Chirodynamics regarding barbed hooks in right-to-left writing (Fig. 94).

120

Fig. 94 The cursive *ayin* is the natural outcome of writing the Square version in one stroke.

*péh*

*péh sophit*

In Part II (p. 71) we saw how the cursive *péh* is essentially the same as its traditional Square form, only rounded and turned upside down (because spirals don't come naturally the other way).

The Square form of *péh sophit* (terminal *péh*) continues the familiar theme of terminal letters extending below the baseline. The coincidental resemblance to a capital *F* – in which the middle horizontal is suspended from the top rather than connected to the stem – is more apparent in the traditional typefaces (far right) than in modern sans-serif ones where the "suspender" is of comparable thickness to the horizontal ending.

How the cursive *péh sophit* came about is more readily compre-hended when placed side by side with its Square versions. The "turnback" loop at the top was incidental (the result of the barbed hook rule working upside down), as was the one at the bottom: the main intention is the long upstroke, which turns around and finishes with a downstroke toward itself.

## *tzadi*

$3 \; \text{צ} \; \text{צ}$

## *tzadi sophit*

$9 \; \text{ץ} \; \text{ץ}$

The Square Hebrew *tzadi* (top right, and Fig. 95-a) is by nature a two-stroke character. Attempting it in one continuous stroke (Fig. 95-b) meant that the top half was now an inverted rainbow arc. Inverted or no, rainbow arcs are only comfortable when hand, slant, and direction of writing are in agreement (Fifth Rule), so the character soon righted itself and evolved into its *3*-like cursive that we know today (Fig. 95-c).

Fig. 95          The birth of the cursive *tzadi*

The same applies to the terminal form (Fig. 96-a). When the mirror *y*-like form was reversed (Fig. 96-b) – the better to suit the hand's natural slant – it became quickly apparent that drawing it like a standard Roman *y* went against the direction of writing, so it made more sense to draw it from the bottom up (Fig. 96-c) – like the *lamed* and *péh sophit*. Finally, it was raised above the baseline, to ensure a reasonably consistent placement. Along the way, the chirodynamics of barbed hooks kicked in, and the loop developed of its own accord.

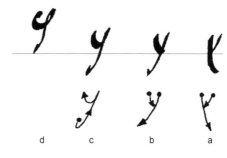

Fig. 96                    Evolution of the *tzadi sophit*

---

**quf**

קקק

Self-explanatory.

---

**resh**

ררר

Self-explanatory.

---

**shin**

ששׁ

See discussion of the cursive letter (p. 87).

---

**tav**

תתת

Self-explanatory.

123

## Putting it all together

To finish, here is the passage from the book of Genesis, chapter 11 that has accompanied us throughout the book, in the Square Hebrew typeface, and with the explicit pointing and cantillations (additional markings, indicating how the text should be sung by the cantor) with which it is normally associated.

וַיְהִי כָל־הָאָרֶץ שָׂפָה אֶחָת וּדְבָרִים אֲחָדִים: וַיְהִי בְּנָסְעָם
מִקֶּדֶם וַיִּמְצְאוּ בִקְעָה בְּאֶרֶץ שִׁנְעָר וַיֵּשְׁבוּ שָׁם: וַיֹּאמְרוּ
אִישׁ אֶל־רֵעֵהוּ הָבָה נִלְבְּנָה לְבֵנִים וְנִשְׂרְפָה לִשְׂרֵפָה
וַתְּהִי לָהֶם הַלְּבֵנָה לְאָבֶן וְהַחֵמָר הָיָה לָהֶם לַחֹמֶר:
וַיֹּאמְרוּ הָבָה ׀ נִבְנֶה־לָּנוּ עִיר וּמִגְדָּל וְרֹאשׁוֹ בַשָּׁמַיִם
וְנַעֲשֶׂה־לָּנוּ שֵׁם פֶּן־נָפוּץ עַל־פְּנֵי כָל־הָאָרֶץ:

Fig. 97  First verses of chapter 11, book of Genesis, in traditional Square Hebrew
(with explicit pointing)

◊

124

## Afterword

Ultimately, any method that makes learning a new writing system easier is to be welcomed. In one of Rudyard Kipling's *Just So Stories*, the alphabet is invented by a little girl in Neolithic times, based on the images in her mind as her father made various sounds, starting with an open-mouthed carp's head for *A*.

While chirodynamics and the history of writing cannot compete with the charm of such tales, they do provide a secure and consistent "scaffolding" with which to build one's knowledge of the subject. If you know of a different set of coordinates or mnemonic aids with which to conquer the Hebrew script more effectively, go for it. Any comprehensive scheme is better than when there is no familiar frame of reference whatsoever. Even with the take-it-or-leave-it method of most conventional HFL studies, the brain eventually creates its own network of mental associations out of the mass of seemingly arbitrary symbols. But it is a haphazard affair – like a fishing net made out of discarded hair nets – and this is reflected in the handwriting of most students who learn the script as adults.

If the method set out within these pages enables you – as it did for my informal students – to shed your intimidation of the script, and to write your name and common English or European words in passable cursive Hebrew, I shall regard my effort as being worthwhile. If, in addition, it has made the Old Testament more accessible and you are able to make out, or spell, key words or place names from the Bible in the original, who can say but that we have made the first steps back to the plain in the land of Shin'ar?

(Wherever that is.)

◊

## Appendix: Transliterated Hebrew for Practice

### [A] Single words

The following words are mostly of foreign (European) origin. In addition to being familiar, they have the virtue of being spelled phonetically in Hebrew, i.e., no knowledge of Hebrew word roots is required, and they obey the consistent rules for terms of foreign origin discussed at the end of Step 3. However, to reiterate the accepted Hebrew spelling (particularly in words where the initial vowel is carried by an *aleph*, e.g., *Aoqtobr* = October), they are transliterated literally in the first column – to wit:

- The letter *aleph* is indicated by *A*

- *o*, *u* and *v* are represented by a plain *vav*

- The *v* sound is represented by *vav* – unless the rules of Hebrew grammar allow a *v*-sounding soft *bet* to be used

- Plain *h* means *héh;* H stands for *Het (*pronounced like the Spanish *j)*

- plain *s* indicates a *sammeç;* *sh* or *s̲* mean a *shin* is used

- *tz* indicates a *tzadi*

- *q* indicates a *quf*

- T stands for *Tet;* plain *t* (representing *th* in the original) is *tav*

Where it appears, the apostrophe following the letters *g*, *z* and *tz* should be duplicated (in mirror fashion) in the Hebrew; it converts these

127

letters to the foreign sounds *j, zh* (as in *beige*), and *tch*, respectively.

As an opportunity to introduce some real Hebrew, a few native words are also included because they are part of the common Judeo-Christian vocabulary (*amen, haleluya*), their Anglicized forms have entered the English lexicon (*Hutzpah, shibolet, leviatan*), they are part of common Jewish culture (*Hanucah, Hupah*), or they are of interest to the Christian reader (*cneisiah* = church, *kineret* = Sea of Galilee). However, none of the words feature the letter *ayin*.

A pronunciation guide is provided in the second column. Reminder:

- All vowels are as in Italian or Spanish.
- Stress is indicated by **boldface** type.
- All instances of plain *g* (i.e., without an apostrophe) are hard.
- *ç* indicates a soft *caf*, pronounced like the German or Scottish *ch* in *Bach* or *loch*.

## *aleph*

| Hebrew transliteration | Pronunciation | Meaning |
|---|---|---|
| *AbsTrqtzih* | *abs**traq**tzia* | abstraction |
| *AdminisTrtzih* | *adminis**tra**tzia* | administration |
| *AgoAisT* | *e**go**ist* | egotist |
| *Amn* | *a**men*** | amen |
| *AogusT* | ***o**gust* | August |
| *AolimpiAdh* | *olimpi**a**da* | Olympic games |

128

## *aleph*

| Hebrew transliteration | Pronunciation | Meaning |
|---|---|---|
| *A o q T o b r* | *oqtober* | October |
| *A o T o b u s* | *otobus* | bus |
| *A o T o m T i* | *otomati* | automatic |
| *A t l T i* | *atleti* | athletic |
| *A T m o s p r h* | *atmosphera* | atmosphere |
| *A u l T i m T u m* | *ultimatum* | ultimatum |
| *A u n i b r s i T h* | *universita* | university |

## *bet*

| Hebrew transliteration | Pronunciation | Meaning |
|---|---|---|
| *b T o n* | *beton* | concrete |
| *b i b l i o g r p i h* | *bibliografia* | bibliography |
| *b i l i A r d* | *biliard* | billiards, pool |
| *b i sho f* | *bishof* | bishop [church] |
| *b i s q v i T* | *bisqvit* | biscuit |
| *b l o n d i n i* | *blondini* | blond [m.] |
| *b n n h* | *banana* | banana |
| *b o h m i* | *bohemi* | bohemian |
| *b o m b s T i* | *bombasti* | bombastic |
| *b o T n i q h* | *botaniqa* | botany |

## *bet*

| Hebrew transliteration | Pronunciation | Meaning |
| --- | --- | --- |
| *bsis* | ***basis*** | basis, base |
| *budhizm* | ***budizm*** | Buddhism |
| *buTiq* | ***butiq*** | boutique |

## *gimmel*

| Hebrew transliteration | Pronunciation | Meaning |
| --- | --- | --- |
| *g'ing'i* | ***gingy*** | redhead |
| *g'irph* | *jirafa* | giraffe |
| *gAogrpih* | *geografia* | geography |
| *gAologih* | *geologia* | geology |
| *girosqop* | *giroscop* | gyroscope |
| *glrih* | *galeria* | gallery |
| *gnrTor* | *generator* | generator |
| *gnTiqh* | *genetiqa* | genetics |
| *gondolh* | ***gondola*** | gondola |
| *goti* | ***goti*** | Gothic |
| *grbiTtzih* | *gravitatzia* | gravity |
| *grgoriAni* | *gregoryani* | Gregorian |
| *grpiqh* | *grafiqa* | graphics |
| *gz* | *gaz* | natural gas |

130

## *dalet*

| Hebrew transliteration | Pronunciation | Meaning |
|---|---|---|
| *dAodornT* | *deodorant* | deodorant |
| *dh pAqTo* | *de facto* | de facto |
| *diATh* | *dieta* | diet |
| *digiTli* | *digitali* | digital |
| *dinmi* | *dinami* | dynamic |
| *dinozAur* | *dinozaur* | dinosaur |
| *diplomT* | *diplomat* | diplomat |
| *diqTTor* | *diqtator* | dictator |
| *dirqTor* | *direqtor* | director |
| *disqrTi* | *disqreti* | discreet |
| *disTAns* | *distans* | at arm's length |
| *dizl* | *dizel* | diesel |
| *dmoqrTih* | *demoqratia* | democracy |
| *dogmh* | *dogma* | dogma |
| *dolpin* | *dolfin* | dolphin |
| *dominnTi* | *dominanti* | dominant |
| *domino* | *domino* | dominoes |
| *doqTor* | *doqtor* | Dr. [title] |
| *ducs* | *ducas* | duke |

## *héh*

| Hebrew transliteration | Pronunciation | Meaning |
|---|---|---|
| *hdonizm* | *hedonizm* | hedonism |
| *hgmonih* | *hegemonia* | hegemony |
| *hidrAuli* | *hidrauli* | hydraulic |
| *higiinh* | *higyena* | hygiene |
| *hiirArcih* | *hirarçia* | hierarchy |
| *hipnozh* | *hipnoza* | hynopsis |
| *hipotizh* | *hipoteza* | hypothesis |
| *hisTorih* | *historia* | history |
| *hisTrih* | *histeria* | hysteria |
| *hlluih* | *haleluya* | hallelujah |
| *homogni* | *homogeni* | homogenous |
| *horosqop* | *horosqop* | horoscope |
| *hroAi* | *heroi* | heroic |
| *humniTri* | *humanitari* | humanitarian |
| *humor* | *humor* | humor |

## *vav*

| Hebrew transliteration | Pronunciation | Meaning |
|---|---|---|
| *vidAo* | *video* | video |
| *vilh* | *vila* | detached house, villa |
| *virus* | *virus* | virus |

## *vav*

| Hebrew transliteration | Pronunciation | Meaning |
|---|---|---|
| *viTmin* | *vitamin* | vitamin |
| *vizh* | *viza* | visa |
| *vizuAli* | *vizuali* | visual |
| *vnil* | *vanil* | vanilla |
| *volT* | *volt* | volt |
| *vTo* | *veto* | veto |
| *vulgri* | *vulgari* | vulgar |
| *vvisqi* | *wisqi* | whiskey |

## *zayin*

| Hebrew transliteration | Pronunciation | Meaning |
|---|---|---|
| *z'qT* | *z'aqet* | jacket |
| *z'rgon* | *z'argon* | jargon |
| *zbrh* | *zebra* | zebra |
| *zig-zg* | *zigzag* | zig-zag |
| *zuAologih* | *zuologia* | zoology |

## *Het*

| Hebrew transliteration | Pronunciation | Meaning |
|---|---|---|
| *Hnuch* | *Hanuca* | Hanukkah |

133

## Het

| Hebrew transliteration | Pronunciation | Meaning |
| --- | --- | --- |
| *Hulign* | *Huligan* | hooligan |
| *Humus* | *Humus* | humus [culin.] |
| *HunTh* | *Hunta* | junta |
| *Huph* | *Hupah* | wedding canopy |
| *Hutzph* | *Hutzpah* | insolence, cheek |

## Tet

| Hebrew transliteration | Pronunciation | Meaning |
| --- | --- | --- |
| *Tblh* | *tavla* | table [in document] |
| *Tbq* | *tabaq* | tobacco |
| *Tcnologih* | *teçnologia* | technology |
| *Tiip* | *tayp* | tape, tape-deck |
| *Tip* | *tip* | tip |
| *Tipus* | *tipus* | type, character |
| *Tiron* | *tiron* | rookie |
| *Tlptih* | *telepatia* | telepathy |
| *Tlq* | *talq* | talcum powder |
| *Tlsqop* | *telescop* | telescope |
| *Tlvvizih* | *televizia* | television |
| *ToalT* | *toalet* | toilet [paper] |
| *Tonh* | *tona* | ton |

134

## *Tet*

| Hebrew transliteration | Pronunciation | Meaning |
|---|---|---|
| *Topogrpih* | *topografia* | topography |
| *TosTr* | **toster** | toaster |
| *ToTliTri* | *totalitari* | totalitarian |
| *TTnus* | **tetanus** | tetanus |
| *Tunh* | **tuna** | tuna |
| *Turbinh* | **turbina** | turbine |
| *Turnir* | *turnir* | tournament |
| *Turqiz* | *turqiz* | tourquoise |

## *yod*

| Hebrew transliteration | Pronunciation | Meaning |
|---|---|---|
| *iguAr* | **yaguar** | jaguar |
| *iidish* | **yidish** | Yiddish |
| *inuAr* | **yanuar** | January |
| *iogurT* | **yogurt** | yogurt |
| *iom cipur* | *yom kipur* | Yom Kippur |
| *ipn* | **yapan** | Japan |
| *irdn* | **yarden** | Jordan |
| *ishu* | **yeshu** | Jesus |
| *isrAl* | **yisrael** | Israel |
| *iuli* | **yuli** | July |

## yod

| Hebrew transliteration | Pronunciation | Meaning |
|---|---|---|
| *i u n i* | *yuni* | June |

## caf

| Hebrew transliteration | Pronunciation | Meaning |
|---|---|---|
| *c r T i s* | *cartis* | card |
| *c h n* | *cohen* | Cohen, priest [gener.] |
| *c i m i h* | *çimih* | chemistry |
| *c i p h* | *kipa* | kippa |
| *c l o r* | *çlor* | chlorine |
| *c n i s i h* | *kneisia* | church |
| *c n r t* | *kineret* | Sea of Galilee |
| *c r u b i m* | *kruvim* | cherubim (cherubs) |
| *c o l s T r o l* | *kolesterol* | cholesterol |
| *c o r i A o g r p i h* | *coreografia* | choreography |
| *c r i z m h* | *carizma* | charisma |
| *c r o n o l o g i h* | *çronologia* | chronology |

# *lamed*

| Hebrew transliteration | Pronunciation | Meaning |
|---|---|---|
| *l b n o n* | *levanon* | Lebanon |
| *l g i T i m i* | *legitimi* | legitimate |
| *l g l i* | *legali* | lawful |
| *l i b r l i* | *liberali* | liberal |
| *l i g h* | *liga* | league |
| *l i g i o n* | *ligyon* | Legion |
| *l i m o n* | *limon* | lemon |
| *l i q r* | *liqer* | liqueur |
| *l i T r* | *liter* | liter |
| *l i T u r g i* | *liturgi* | liturgical |
| *l o g i q h* | *logiqa* | logic |
| *l o g i s T i q h* | *logistiqa* | logistics |
| *l o g r i t m* | *logaritm* | logarithm |
| *l o i A l i* | *loyali* | loyal |
| *l o T o* | *loto* | lotto, lottery |
| *l T i n i t* | *latinit* | Latin |
| *l u q s u s* | *luqsus* | luxury |
| *l u t r n i* | *luterani* | Lutheran |
| *l v i* | *levi* | Levy, of Levite clan |
| *l v i t n* | *levyatan* | whale, leviathan |

## *mem*

| Hebrew transliteration | Pronunciation | Meaning |
| --- | --- | --- |
| *m A i* | *Mai* | May |
| *m As T r o* | *maestro* | maestro |
| *m d i T t̲z̲i h* | *meditatzia* | meditation |
| *m d l i h* | *medalia* | medal |
| *m g n T* | *magnet* | magnet |
| *m g n z i u m* | *magnezium* | magnesium |
| *m g z i n* | *magazin* | magazine |
| *m o d l* | *model* | model |
| *m o d r n i* | *moderni* | modern |
| *m o d u l r i* | *modulari* | modular |
| *m o l q u l h* | *molequla* | molecule |
| *m o m n T u m* | *momentum* | momentum |
| *m o n o p o l* | *monopol* | monopoly |
| *m o n o t A i z m* | *monoteizm* | monotheism |
| *m o n o T o n i* | *monotoni* | monotonous |
| *m o T i b t̲z̲i h* | *motivatzia* | motivation |
| *m o z A i q h* | *mozaiqa* | mosaic |
| *m u s i q h* | *musiqa* | music |
| *m u s l m i* | *muslemi* | muslim |
| *m u z i A o n* | *muzeon* | museum |

138

## *nun*

| Hebrew transliteration | Pronunciation | Meaning |
| --- | --- | --- |
| *n A i b i* | *naivi* | naïve |
| *n i i T r l i* | *naytrali* | neutral |
| *n i q o T i n* | *niqotin* | nicotine |
| *n i r v v A n h* | *nirvana* | nirvana |
| *n o b m b r* | *november* | November |
| *n o i r o l o g i h* | *noirologia* | neurology |
| *n o m i n l i* | *nominali* | nominal |
| *n o q A A u T* | *noqaut* | knockout |
| *n o r m l i* | *normali* | normal |
| *n o r v g i h* | *norvegia* | Norway |
| *n o s T l g i h* | *nostalgia* | nostalgia |
| *n o T r i o n* | *notaryon* | notary public |
| *n o t̲z̲ r i* | *notzri* | Christian |
| *n t̲z̲ r t* | *natzeret / natzrat* | Nazereth |
| *n u A n s* | *nuans* | nuance |
| *n u d n i q* | *nudniq* | nag, nuisance |

## *sammeç*

| Hebrew transliteration | Pronunciation | Meaning |
| --- | --- | --- |
| *s i m u l T n i* | *simultani* | simultaneous |
| *s i T u A t̲z̲ i h* | *situatzia* | situation |

## *sammeç*

| Hebrew transliteration | Pronunciation | Meaning |
|---|---|---|
| *sodh* | *soda* | soda |
| *solidriut* | *solidariut* | solidarity |
| *solo* | *solo* | solo |
| *sonATh* | *sonata* | sonata |
| *sotziAli* | *sotzyali* | social |
| *sTirh* | *satira* | satire |
| *sTndrTi* | *standarti* | standard [adj.] |
| *sTrili* | *sterili* | sterile |
| *sTrio* | *stereo* | stereo |
| *sTTisTiqh* | *statistiqa* | statistics |
| *sTTus* | *status* | status |
| *sTudnT* | *student* | student |
| *subiiqTibi* | *subyeqtivi* | subjective |
| *subsidih* | *subsidia* | subsidy |
| *sub-Tropi* | *sub-tropi* | subtropical |
| *sucot* | *Sucot* | Succoth |
| *sucr* | *sucar* | sugar |
| *suriAlizm* | *surealizm* | surrealism |
| *suuiTh* | *suita* | suite |
| *svvdr* | *sveder* | sweater |

## *péh*

| Hebrew transliteration | Pronunciation | Meaning |
| --- | --- | --- |
| *pbruAr* | *februar* | February |
| *pdgog* | *pedagog* | pedagog |
| *pdrli* | *federali* | federal |
| *polish* | *polisa* | insurance policy |
| *poliTiqh* | *politiqa* | politics |
| *polqlor* | *folklor* | folklore |
| *ponTi* | *foneti* | phonetic |
| *popqorn* | *popqoren* | popcorn |
| *populri* | *populari* | popular |
| *pormli* | *formali* | formal |
| *porum* | *forum* | forum |
| *poTntziAli* | *potentzyal* | potential |
| *poTogni* | *fotogeni* | photogenic |
| *pozh* | *poza* | pose, affectation |
| *proshi* | *proshi* | Pharisee |
| *pudl* | *pudel* | poodle |
| *punqtzih* | *funqtzia* | function |
| *purim* | *Purim* | Purim |
| *puriTni* | *puritani* | puritan |

## *tzadi*

| Hebrew transliteration | Pronunciation | Meaning |
| --- | --- | --- |
| *tz'lo* | *tchello* | cello |
| *tz'rTr* | *tcharter* | charter |
| *tzbr* | *tzabar* | sabra [native Israeli] |
| *tzdoqi* | *tzdoqi* | Sadducee |
| *tzilindr* | *tzilinder* | cylinder |
| *tzini* | *tzini* | cynical |
| *tzion* | *tzion* | Zion |
| *tziviliztzih* | *tzivilizatzia* | civilization |
| *tzlzius* | *tzelzius* | Celsius |
| *tznTripugh* | *tzentrifuga* | centrifuge |
| *tznzurh* | *tzenzura* | censorship |

## *quf*

| Hebrew transliteration | Pronunciation | Meaning |
| --- | --- | --- |
| *qAuboi* | *kauboi* | cowboy |
| *qbinT* | *kabinet* | Cabinet [gov.] |
| *qdntzih* | *kadentzia* | term [gov.] |
| *qibutz* | *kibutz* | kibbutz |
| *qiosq* | *kiosq* | kiosk |
| *qisr* | *keisar* | emperor, Caesar |
| *qlibr* | *kaliber* | caliber |

## *quf*

| Hebrew transliteration | Pronunciation | Meaning |
| --- | --- | --- |
| *qliinT* | *kliyent* | client |
| *qliniqh* | *kliniqa* | clinic |
| *qolgʿ* | *kolej* | college |
| *qombintzih* | *kombinatzia* | combination |
| *qomdih* | *komedia* | comedy |
| *qongrs* | *kongres* | Congress |
| *qoniAq* | *koniaq* | Cognac |
| *qonqrTi* | *konqreti* | concrete [adj.] |
| *qonsul* | *konsul* | consul |
| *qontzrT* | *kontzert* | concert |
| *qoTgʿ* | *kotej* | cottage cheese, town-house |
| *qtoli* | *katoli* | Catholic |
| *qTsTroph* | *katastrofa* | catastrophe |

## *resh*

| Hebrew transliteration | Pronunciation | Meaning |
| --- | --- | --- |
| *rb* | *rav* | rabbi |
| *rdiATor* | *radyator* | radiator |
| *rdiqli* | *radikali* | radical |
| *rdius* | *radius* | radius |
| *riAlisTi* | *realisti* | realistic |

## *resh*

| Hebrew transliteration | Pronunciation | Meaning |
|---|---|---|
| *rlvvAnTi* | *relevanti* | relevant |
| *roboT* | *robot* | robot |
| *romAi* | *romai* | Roman |
| *romnTi* | *romanti* | romantic |
| *roTtzih* | *rotatzia* | rotation |
| *rpormh* | *reforma* | reform |
| *rprTuAr* | *repertuar* | repertoire |
| *rpubliqni* | *republikani* | Republican |
| *rsiTl* | *resital* | recital |
| *rTroAqTibi* | *retroaktivi* | retroactive |
| *rtzionli* | *ratzionali* | rational |
| *rvizionisT* | *revizionist* | Revisionist |
| *rvvrs* | *revers* | reverse |
| *rzrbh* | *rezerva* | reserve |

## *shin*

| Hebrew transliteration | Pronunciation | Meaning |
|---|---|---|
| *shbt* | *shabat* | Shabbat, Sabbath |
| *srpim* | *srafim* | seraphim |
| *shibolt* | *shibolet* | shibboleth |
| *shlom* | *shalom* | peace / hello / goodbye |

144

## *shin*

| Hebrew transliteration | Pronunciation | Meaning |
| --- | --- | --- |
| *shmpnih* | *shampania* | champagne |
| *shnitzl* | *shnitzel* | schnitzl |
| *shnorql* | *shnorkel* | snorkel |
| *shomrom* | *shomron* | Samaria |
| *shoqold* | *shoqolad* | chocolate |

## *tav*

| Hebrew transliteration | Pronunciation | Meaning |
| --- | --- | --- |
| *tAologih* | *teologia* | theology |
| *tAorih* | *teoria* | theory |
| *tiATron* | *tiatron* | theater |
| *tizh* | *teza* | thesis |
| *tlmud* | *Talmud* | Talmud |
| *tnc* | *Tanaç* | Old Testament |
| *torh* | *Torah* | Torah, Pentateuch |
| *trApih* | *terapia* | therapy |
| *trmos* | *termos* | thermos flask |

◊

145

## Notes

1   S. Haramati, *Halaçah Uma'aseh Behora'at Halashon Ha'ivrit* [Theory and Practice in Hebrew Language Teaching] Tel-Aviv, 1968. The author, sometime senior official at the Ministry of Education and central in formulating much of the Hebrew studies curriculum in Israeli schools, advocates teaching students to write Hebrew before they learn to read it:

> (in contrast to the modern approach)... in order to provide for a change in the type of practice (from speech to writing) and to allow the students a measure of kinetic activity (of the hand muscles), as these factors (variety and student participation) will considerably help speed up the learning process. (p. 27)

Furthermore, he states that "when teaching [Hebrew to] adults there is no point in teaching how to write in print ("Square") letters, as they will not be required to use these in practice." (p. 208).

2   For an example of Moses brandishing tablets with Square Hebrew inscriptions, see: http://www.abcgallery.com/R/rembrandt/rembrandt132.html

3   J. Naveh, *Early History of the Alphabet*, Jerusalem, 1982, p.123, quoting the Babylonian Talmud, Sanhedrin 21b.

4   J. Naveh, *ibid*, p.123.

5   M. Landman, *Tiqun Hactav Ha'ivri*, Jerusalem 1979, pp 53-54, 144; and E. Raizen, *Romanization of the Hebrew Script: Ideology, Attempts and Failure*, Austin, 1987, pp. iv-v, 64-65, 69.

6   A. Gaur, *A History of Writing*, London (Revised Ed.) 1992, pp. 53, 54.

7    S. Haramati, p. 233.

8    René Ponot, as quoted by Georges Jean in *Writing – The Story of Alphabets and Scripts*, London 1992, provides a vivid description of the evolution of the Roman aesthetic as follows:

> 'The inscription... no longer at eye-level, became therefore larger and more deeply cut into the stone. Even when tinted with colour, the grooves of the letters were rendered legible through the use of light and shade cast at different angles onto the lines. Rainwater gradually removed the colour from the vertical parts, leaving these less easily visible, while at the same time the horizontal lines became more pronounced as they caught and retained dirt...

> 'If the letters were to retain their uniform appearance, some alterations in their proportions had to be made. This was only possible by making the horizontal lines thinner than the verticals...'

9    A. Even-Shoshan, *Lashon Uçtav* [Language and Script], Jerusalem, 1961, pp. 154-162.

◊

# Bibliography / Further Reading

*Titles marked with an asterisk (\*) appear in both European (English/French) and Hebrew editions – occasionally in the same volume. In these cases, the European title only is listed.  Hebrew titles are listed in their Hebrew alphabetical order.*

## English/French/Latin Sources

- Beit-Arié, Malachi, *Specimens of Mediaeval Hebrew Scripts*,\* Jerusalem, 1988
- Beit-Arié, Malachi, *The Makings of the Medieval Hebrew Book*, Jerusalem 1993
- Birnbaum, Solomon A., *The Hebrew Script* (Vol. I and II), Jerusalem, 1971
- Chayen, M.J., *The Phonetics of Modern Hebrew*, Paris, 1973
- Davies, Martin, *Aldus Manutius: Printer and Publisher of Renaissance Venice*, London, 1995
- Davies, W.V., *Egyptian Hieroglyphics*, Reading the Past, London, 1987
- Day, Lewis F., *Alphabets Old and New*, London, 1995
- Diringer, D., *The Alphabet* (Vol. I), London, 1968
- Driver, G.R., *Semitic Writing* (second ed.), London, 1954
- Gaur, Albertine, *A History of Writing* (revised ed.), London, 1992

- Hadas-Lebel, Mireille, *Histoire de la langue hébraïque*, Paris, 1957
- Haley, Allan, *Alphabet – The History, Evolution and Design of the Letters We Use Today*, London 1995
- Harris, Roy, *The Origin of Writing*, London, 1986
- Jean, Georges, *Writing: The Story of Alphabets and Scripts,* trans. Jenny Oates, London, 1992
- Naveh, Joseph, *Early History of the Alphabet,*\* Jerusalem, 1982
- Nesbitt, Alexander, *The History and Technique of Lettering*, New York, 1957
- Pinker, Steven, *The Language Instinct*, 1994
- Raizen, Esther, *Romanization of the Hebrew Script: Ideology, Attempts & Failure*, Austin, 1987
- Weiser, Rafael, *Books from Sepharad,*\* Jerusalem, 1992
- Wolf, Jo. Christoph. II, *Bibliothecæ Hebræ* (Vol. III), Hamburg and Leipzig, 1527

## Hebrew Sources

- Even-Shoshan, Avraham, *Lashon Uçtav* [Language and Script], Jerusalem, 1961
- Beit-Arié, Malachi, *Meqorot Leqodiqologia Vepaleographia Ivrit* [Sources of Hebrew Codicology and Paleography], ed. Tamar Leiter, Jerusalem, 1994
- Gonen, Rivka, *Toldot Hactav Ha-ivri* [History of the Hebrew Script], Jerusalem, 1970

149

- Diringer, David, *Ha'encyclopedia Ha'ivrit* [The Hebrew Encyclopedia] (Vol. 20), s.v. *ctav* [script], Jerusalem, 1971, pp.1094-1107

- Haramati, Shlomo, *Halaçah Uma'aseh Behora'at Halashon Ha'ivrit* [Theory and Practice in Hebrew Language Teaching], Tel-Aviv, 1968

- Tur-Sinai, Naftali H., *Encyclopedia Miqraït* [The Biblical Encyclopedia] (Vol. 1), s.v. *alefbet* [alphabet], Jerusalem, 1950, pp. 372-415

- Yardeni, Ada, *Sefer Hactav Ha'ivri* [The Book of the Hebrew Script], Jerusalem, 1991

- Landman, Michael, *Tiqun Hactav Ha'ivri* [Reforming the Hebrew Script], Jerusalem, 1979

- Naveh, Yosef, *Otiot Vetoldoteihen* [Letters and Their History], Jerusalem, 1979

- Kassuto, M.D. and Licht, Y.S., *Encyclopedia Miqraït* (Vol. 4), s.v. *ctav uçtiva* [script and writing], Jerusalem, 1962, pp. 372-377

- Rabin, Haïm, *Encyclopedia Miqraït* (Vol. 6), s.v. *ivrit* [Hebrew], Jerusalem, 1971, pp. 51-73

- Rabin, Haïm, *Iqarei Toldot Halashon Ha'ivrit* [Outline History of the Hebrew Language], Jerusalem, 1972

◊

## Index

Made in the USA
San Bernardino, CA
23 April 2020